MICHIGAN'S BEST

OUTDOOR ADVENTURES WITH CHILDREN

Jim DuFresne

The Mountaineers/Seattle

To Michael and Jessica.
Because the small footprints in the dunes
blow away so quickly.

The Mountaineers: Organized 1906 "... *to explore, study, preserve, and enjoy the natural beauty of the outdoors.*"

4 3 2 1 0
5 4 3 2 1

Published by The Mountaineers
306 Second Avenue West, Seattle, Washington 98119
Published simultaneously in Canada by Douglas & McIntyre, Ltd., 1615 Venables Street, Vancouver, B.C. V5L 2H1
Manufactured in the United States of America

Edited by Joan C. Gregory
Maps by Newell Cartographics
Cover photographs: Bottom left courtesy Michigan Travel Bureau. All other photos by Jim DuFresne.
All other photographs by the author
Book design and layout by Bridgett Culligan

Library of Congress Cataloging-in-Publication Data

DuFresne, Jim.
    Michigan's best outdoor adventures with children / Jim DuFresne.
        p.   cm.
    Includes bibliographical references and index.
    ISBN 0-89886-249-3
    1. Outdoor recreation for children--Michigan--Guide-books.
    2. Hiking--Michigan--Guide-books. 3. Trails--Michigan--Guide-books.
    4. Camping--Michigan--Guide-books. 5. Canoes and canoeing-
    -Michigan--Guide-books. 6. Michigan--Description and travel--1981-
    --Guide-books. I. Mountaineers (Society) II. Title.
    GV191.63.D84   1990
    796.5'09774--dc20   90-37450
                                                             CIP

CONTENTS

LEGEND

••••	ROUTE	⊼	PICNIC AREA
– ᵔ – –	OTHER TRAIL	⊞	TOILET
‿ ⋯ –	STREAM	◣◢	VIEWPOINT
⌂	CAMPGROUND	≝≝	MARSH

FOREWORD

Whatever the season or wherever travelers might find themselves in Michigan, adventure is just around the corner.

That's especially truc when experiencing the outdoors with youngsters. They don't need much—a modest trail, a final destination, a pack with a few treats, and a spirit of fun supplied with a smile from mom and dad.

Jim DuFresne has been traipsing around Michigan's natural highlights with his youngsters for some time now, writing about his experiences for *The Saginaw News* and seven other Booth newspapers in the state. His collection of some of his favorite trips deserves a place on bookshelves—or better yet in backpacks—of all parents who like to share outdoor experiences with their children.

In addition to his knowledge about the outdoors, Jim's love for having fun with his children is obvious.

If you have the book, you've taken the first step. The next one takes a little more effort.

Get out and enjoy some Michigan adventures with your children. Years from now, your youngsters will cherish the special times you had together.

Ken Tabacsko, Feature Editor
The Saginaw News

ACKNOWLEDGMENTS

After three years of venturing into the woods, it finally happened at the end of Jessica's sixth summer. While I was tying her younger brother's shoes on a trail in Sleeping Bear Dunes National Lakeshore, Jessica announced she was going to start back to camp . . . on her own. She quickly climbed over a low, wooded dune, hiked 50 yards down the trail, and then suddenly realized that nothing surrounded her but trees . . . no signs, no buildings, no other people, no daddy.

It was probably the first time she had ever been in the woods all by herself, and it was a little scary. So Jessica sat down in the middle of the trail and sang to herself until we came walking over the dune.

"I decided I better wait to make sure you guys were all right."

I suppressed my smile, told her everything was fine, and then asked her if she could lead us back to camp. My daughter immediately took her position at the front and marched off, the proudest trail leader I've seen.

Kids—they're as natural in the outdoors as they are in a Saturday matinee. After many grand wilderness adventures around the world—scaling peaks, walking glaciers, and running wild water—I've concentrated the past few years on showing my children a slice of Michigan along short trails, on overnight backpacking trips, and on calm lakes. Reaching a 12,000-foot pass in New Zealand is fine, but I've never regretted a moment spent observing a deer with my daughter or seeing the excitement burst from my son after he's lifted his Mickey Mouse fishing rod and discovered a small bluegill on his hook.

If children have slowed me down, it was only to observe things I have missed too often in my hurry to reach the peak.

I deeply appreciate all the assistance from my editors at The Mountaineers Books, who encouraged me to write this book, as well as the editors at the *Saginaw News* and the *Booth*

News Service in Lansing, who launched my statewide column, "Kidventures." Others, like Sandy Graham at the Benchmark—a parent with his own backpacking children— Jean Bergerson at The Great Outdoors of Minnesota, and Dana Grover at Sawyer Canoes, have contributed significantly to this project, as have numerous rangers at Michigan's national parks and forests, and managers at state parks who alerted me to many of these wonderfully short adventures.

Most of all, these summers couldn't have been possible without the help of Jessica and Michael DuFresne, Kyle Clarkson, and all the other children I walked or paddled behind.

■ A NOTE ABOUT SAFETY

Safety is an important concern in all outdoor activities. No guidebook can alert you to every hazard or anticipate the limitations of every reader. Therefore, the descriptions of roads, trails, routes, and natural features in this book are not representations that a particular place or excursion will be safe for your party. When you follow any of the routes described in this book, you assume responsibility for your own safety. Under normal conditions, such excursions require the usual attention to traffic, road and trail conditions, weather, terrain, the capabilities of your party, and other factors. Keeping informed on current conditions and exercising common sense are the keys to a safe, enjoyable outing.

The Mountaineers

▌INTRODUCTION

■ Somebody gave me a nudge and I lazily opened my eyes and lifted my head. It was my daughter and she said, "Dad, the beach is ours again."

So it was. The pair of hikers who had appeared briefly at the other end were gone. Once again Jessica and I were the only occupants on this long stretch of sand that bordered the turquoise waters of Lake Michigan and looked toward sand dunes towering in the distance.

It was quite a place, and on this late August afternoon, it was all ours. We were on an island paradise, and from the beach it could have passed easily for a remote spot in the South Pacific. But we had never left Michigan. I discovered South Manitou Island when I went searching for little adventures. My then five-year-old daughter had been car camping but never backpacking. This was her first experience at hiking into a campground with some gear on her back and I wanted to make sure it was a good one. Her pack had to be light, which meant mine was going to be heavy. Small price to pay for a happy camper. The hike had to be short, no more than 2 miles to our destination.

But most of all, it had to be adventurous enough to keep her mind off weary legs. South Manitou Island fit the bill nicely and eventually I discovered many special places in Michigan do. Looking to expose your children to the outdoors? Michigan is a great state to do it. The opportunities for short hikes, gentle canoe trips, and level ski routes are almost unlimited.

The seventy-five adventures compiled in this book were chosen because they represent a variety of activities and a wide range of physical challenges for children, from easy strolls to climbs to commanding views. But most of all, these trips cover the best scenery Michigan, a state blessed with a treasure of natural jewels, has to offer. That's the key. It's not enough just to choose a short, level trail for a youngster's first hike. It's better to choose a longer one if it includes viewing a shipwreck, walking a section along a lakeshore, or watching frogs leap into a marshland. Keep the mind active and the legs never tire as quickly.

These adventures are geared for children ages three to ten. With a good child carrier, infants five months or older can be part of many of these hikes, while toddlers under the age of three will also enjoy the scenic drives and viewpoints (see index for adventures by age), where little or no physical activity is involved. But it's been my experience that most children are ready to begin easy 1- or 2-mile hikes after they are three.

By the time they reach adolescence, ages ten to thirteen, children can work up to hikes of 9 to 10 miles, with the proper pretrip conditioning and mild days at the beginning of each expedition. Many will be able to paddle for 45 minutes to an hour at a stretch, or carry not only their personal gear in a backpack but a share of the group equipment. At this point, for all practical purposes, children can join their parents on almost any outing in Michigan. That makes the three-to-ten-year age period crucial in developing an appreciation, even a never-ending love, for the outdoors and non-motorized adventures.

Setting an agreeable pace on the trail is important, but most unsuccessful family outings result from poor planning, not fast walking. You need to study the proposed adventure carefully, the mileage involved each day, the type of terrain that will be covered, and other factors, such as "Will it be buggy?" Then look at the younger members of your party and decide whether they can handle the journey comfortably.

■ HOW TO USE THIS BOOK

Each adventure begins with a trip synopsis—a block of information that shows at a glance the type of activity, the location, the distance that will be hiked, skied, or paddled, and where to call for more information. Most of the time, a quick look will tell you if this is the outing you are looking for.

By far the most important category is "Difficulty," in which each adventure is rated as "easy," "moderate," or "challenging." Because children grow at different rates and develop coordination and motor skills at different times of their youth, they could be anywhere in a wide range of ages before they could undertake a "moderate" or "challenging" level of physical endurance. To successfully introduce the outdoors to children, it's crucial to know your child's limits and abilities. I've seen some five-year-olds tackle 6 rugged miles on Isle Royale National Park and others who are drained after a walk around the block.

Easy: Most of these hikes and backpacking trips range

Backpacker, Porcupine Mountains Wilderness State Park

from 1 to 2 miles a day. The terrain is predominately level, provides easy footing, and can be handled by most children ages three to five. At this age children have a short attention span, so adventures with a variety of scenery have been selected. Many are interpretive trails, with numbered posts that correspond to information in brochures, an excellent choice for a child's first hike. Plan on frequent stops and more than an hour to cover a level mile of trail with a three-year-old.

Moderate: The physical endurance, motor skills, and attention span has improved greatly for children ages six to eight, and most should be able to handle a moderate-rated trip. Hikes and backpacking adventures in this category range from 3 to 5 miles, but parents still need to plan numerous snack and water breaks for short rests, as well as a long lunch break. Children can also handle steeper climbs, especially some of the sand dune country on the west side of the state. They usually love sitting in the front of a canoe and working a paddle, but don't expect a steady series of strokes from them.

Challenging: Children who are nine to ten years old are capable, with proper conditioning, of covering 6- to 8-mile hikes or steep grades to high points like those found in Porcupine Mountains Wilderness State Park. They are also quite agreeable to spending numerous days in a tent away from home, making a week-long adventure to Isle Royale National Park possible. Regardless of age, all children are intrigued by wildlife and the natural world around them, but at this stage they are old enough to visualize the course on a map, keep track of miles, and pace themselves mentally to reach a goal like a trailside camp at the end of a day.

Each trip synopsis is followed by a description of the adventure itself—not every foot of the trail, but steep climbs to consider, panoramas not to be missed, and points of interest to ponder for a minute or two. The text also describes spots along the route where you can turn around or loop back to shorten the trip, as well as places that make for scenic rest stops or snack breaks. With children, this is important information to have, as the inevitable question during the hike will be "How much farther until we stop for lunch?"

The majority of the outings described also include maps; in many instances, this is the only one you might need. If more detailed maps are desired, you can purchase U.S. Geological Survey 7.5-minute series topographic quads (scale: 1 inch equals 2,000 feet) from the state Department of Natural Resources by contacting DNR Information Services, P.O. Box 30028, Lansing, MI 48909; (517) 373-1220. All Michigan quads are listed in "Michigan Map Coverage," a catalog that can be obtained for free from USGS, Map Distribution, P.O. Box 25286, Denver, CO 80225; (303) 236-7477.

■ TAKING CHILDREN OUTDOORS

DAY HIKING

A simple walk in the woods is often the best start to a lifetime of adventure outdoors. Read about a hike and then use the information to motivate children at the beginning. Tell them you're going to see a waterfall, a lighthouse, trout rising to the surface of a clear stream, or freighters plying the waters of the Great Lakes. A little excitement at the start goes a long way toward motivating young hikers. After that wears off, or after you've passed the shipwreck, be prepared to bribe them with "energy food" (candy and sweet snacks to some people). It's the old carrot-on-the-stick trick. Tell them that in 15 or 20 minutes you'll stop for a snack, and then dole out just enough so there's some left over for the next break.

Children learn quickly that being "the leader" is an important and even prestigious role. The younger hikers should always lead, forcing older members of the party to adjust to their pace. Rotate this title, however, or you might have a major dispute on your hands. Emphasize to the leader and every child in the group the importance of not running, a tendency that is always strong among children, especially those under the age of five. That run-and-stop, run-and-stop pace will wear them out quickly. Tell kids, or even force them if need be, to walk in a slower but steadier stride. Soon they will learn that this is the best way to hike a trail.

Although high-tech hiking boots are available even for toddlers, the vast majority of the trails described in this book do not require such expensive footwear. Sturdy tennis shoes and thick socks are sufficient for the "easy" and "moderate" hikes in this book, and when an adventure needs more than that, it's spelled out clearly in the text. During the summer, bring plenty of energy food, sunscreen, insect repellent, even long-sleeve shirts and pants if it's the height of the bug season (late June to early August). Most important, don't forget the water bottle. Children, especially those under the age of five, are much more vulnerable to heat stress than adults and should drink water often on the trail.

Schedule not only rest stops, snack breaks, and a lunch period, but also time for frequent stops along the trail—to observe ducks in a pond, a spider's web glistening with the morning dew, or a golden mushroom popping through a layer of wet leaves. This is when children learn to appreciate the outdoors and respect their environment. I'm often amazed at the end of an adventure to learn that my son's high point of the day wasn't the view from the top of the ridge, but an inch worm he saw crawling on a leaf.

Pass along your outdoor experience and observations, praise young hikers for how long they've walked or how high they've climbed ... and be patient. Give children the time to inspect and examine this new world around them.

CAMPING

A stroll through any of the modern campgrounds in Michigan provides evidence that families begin taking children camping almost from birth. The Michigan State Park system offers more than 14,000 sites, most of which feature electric hook-ups, showers, heated restrooms, and other such conveniences. Such facilities make a weekend away from home considerably easier for the kids, as well as for mom and dad. A modern campground teaches children the first lesson of camping: It's possible to have fun without television, video recorder, boom box, or toys within arm's reach.

But I prefer taking my children to the rustic campgrounds found in many state parks and scattered throughout the state forests, four national forests, and national parks and lakeshores in Michigan. These are less crowded, feature space and trees instead of recreation vehicles around each site, and create more of a sense that you are outdoors. The most difficult part about such rustic facilities isn't getting children to sleep on the floor of a tent. After a day of fresh air and vigorous activity, most, unlike their parents, nod right

Family on the Dune Climb, Sleeping Bear National Lakeshore

off, even without the aid of sleeping pad. The most difficult part might be getting them to use the vault toilets. Be patient with them when it comes to "toilets with no handle."

For the child who is apprehensive about spending a night in a tent or in the woods, the frontier cabins that can be rented in state parks or the Rent-A-Tipi program is a good way to ease into camping. Especially the tipis, which seem to capture the imagination of children, who spend a weekend fantasizing about the Old West as opposed to worrying about being away from their bedrooms.

When camping, bringing some toys is necessary, especially bedtime Teddy. But don't overload the car by hauling in the toy box. For most young campers, finding a feather on the ground or a grasshopper on a plant will inevitably make up for whatever toy was left at home.

BACKPACKING

Even a three- or four-year-old can go backpacking, if his or her parents are willing to carry the gear in. Place a small daypack on the child's back, stick a coat or another piece of clothing inside that will give the pack some bulk but not much weight, and there will be few problems with an overnight hike into the woods. If a young hiker can undertake a 1- or 2-mile day hike, then a 1-mile walk into a backcountry campground, many of which are described in this book, should be no problem. The important aspect of backpacking is the lesson that you can survive with everything strapped to your back. It doesn't take children long to learn the simplicity of survival. Plus, when they return the next day to see the car (security) still there, they swell with a tremendous sense of accomplishment.

Children in the range of six to eight years of age can begin carrying much of their own gear, as long as their packs don't exceed twenty-five percent of their body weight. They should also be carrying their own water and learning how to ration it over the course of the day. From ages nine to ten, children should be able to carry all their own gear, plus a small portion of group equipment. They should now be able to handle some simple camp tasks on their own, such as gathering firewood, filling up the water bottles, or inserting the stakes in a free-standing tent.

In many ways children are like adults when it comes to backpacking. They need to have raingear, hats, insect repellent, extra clothing, and warm jerseys or sweaters. They get as cold in wet jeans as anybody else, and at dinner time, after hiking 4 miles in the woods, kids are going to be as hungry as you are. The biggest mistake I make with my children is underestimating how much their appetites increase while backpacking. We're forever fighting over the last ravioli in th an.

NOEING

Canoe trips with children can be easy or challeng res. A three-year-old who can't paddle a stroke he outing from a seat in the middle. But a yo ont means the parent in the back has to wo void trees, sweepers, rocks, and other Water trips should either be slow, wi the Huron in southeast Michigan or chains of lakes. Paddling across a lake to a backcountry site, such as those found in Sylvania Recreation Area, is an excellent overnight adventure for kids under the age of five. Kids aren't exerting a lot of energy, don't have to carry a pack, yet can sneak away from all signs of civilization.

Choose the family canoe carefully—a high-sided, long boat (17 feet or more) that is very stable. Equip everybody with a lifejacket and before the first stroke, teach children not to stand, shift their weight suddenly, or reach over the side in an attempt to grab a lily pad. You'll find kids will become restless much quicker sitting in a canoe than hiking, and that more frequent stops are needed for them to get out and stretch their legs. A 3-hour paddle to the campsite, or even less, is ideal for most children on their first overnight canoe trip.

SKIING

Ask any ski instructor, who are the hardest people to teach cross-country skiing? It's the parents, the ones who show up grudgingly the day after Christmas with the new pair of skis that all the kids chipped in and bought. These folks are still, cold, and scared out of their minds. The easiest students? Children, of course, the younger the better.

Kids, especially toddlers, are flexible. That ability to stick their big toe in their mouth is a great asset in skiing. They don't mind falling. Granted, a two-year-old doesn't have nearly as far to go as the parents, and snowsuits and diapers provide plenty of padding, but it's still a mental thing. Kids have no fear. Falling in the snow is fun, which makes learning to ski even more fun. The hardest part of teaching children to ski may be getting their thumbs into the thumb holes of their mittens. The rest is easy.

My children were two years old when we strapped the boots into a pair of "kid's skis." They never used po rst couple winters, as all I wanted them to learn w ings: don't cross the tips, and slide. They had to their skis straight without looking at them a l they had to learn to slide their feet along, r s if they were walking. They practically ha end of the first day.

When my daughter turned five, she moved into a full set of skis with three-pin bindings, boots, and poles. By the end of that winter she was tackling 1- to 2-mile runs, as well as successfully negotiating gentle hills. Like every other activity, children progress on skis at different rates. If you're confronted with the problem of several young skiers and a toddler who can't keep up, use a sled with a back on it and a harness for pulling it. (Known as "Pulks," these can be purchased at any good ski shop. There are several good ones on the market.)

Just remember to bundle up the child riding the sled extra well, as he or she will be more apt to catch cold because of the inactive position. Even the skiers should be dressed in numerous layers. Children are much more vulnerable to getting chilled or even being exposed to hypothermia much sooner than adults (see discussion of hypothermia under Safety).

FISHING

Kids are naturally drawn to fishing, even if they don't have the attention span the sport requires. For that reason it is best to start from the shore or a dock and equip them with a short rod and closed-face reel or even a cane pole. Rig the lines with a good size bobber, some weight, and a hook with whatever bait happens to be available—worms, crickets, or grasshoppers. This set-up will work well with panfish, which is the best species for a young angler to pursue.

The key is to teach them to keep an eye on the bobber and to "set the hook"—a hard upward swing of the rod—when the bobber begins to dip. Not such an easy lesson for a three- or four-year-old to learn. But many of the fishing opportunities described in this book are lakes with good stocks of panfish. A calm evening in mid- to late summer will bring schools of bluegill, sunfish, and pumpkinseed near the shore and a well-placed bobber will be dipping enough to maintain the interest of most children. Catching a big northern pike or walleye is fine, but as far as kids are concerned, hooking a bucketful of perch or panfish is better, even if they are too small to keep.

After a season or two of fishing with a bobber rig, children are often coordinated and interested enough to try casting a small spoon or spinner. At that point, adventures into areas like Sylvania Recreation Area or Big Island Lake Federal Wilderness, where the fishing is exceptionally good at the right time of year, can be rewarding experiences that combine a night on the lakeshore with some fresh fish in the fry pan. Children under the age of sixteen do not need a Michigan fishing license; all others do.

■ THE TEN ESSENTIALS

To take your child on the Marshland Wildlife Drive in Seney National Wildlife Refuge, no essential equipment is needed because you never leave the car. But the vast majority of these adventures are hikes along a trail, a paddle across a lake, or a night in the woods. For activities such as these, The Mountaineers has developed a list of the "Ten Essentials," equipment that should be carried on every major outdoor outing.

1. Extra clothing. Weather can change quickly, and for a child to be caught in a rainstorm without a change of clothing or a jacket could be a serious situation.

2. Extra food. A hungry child is one who plods along making an unexpectedly lengthy hike last even longer.

3. Sunglasses. The sun can be blinding on snow, water, and especially on a windblown sand dune.

4. Knife. No one should go anywhere without a good pocket knife.

5. Firestarter. Either a chemical fuel or even the stub of a candle can be used to start a fire and provide warmth if you have to delay your return.

6. Waterproof matches. The firestarter isn't much good without a way to light it.

7. First-aid kit. It doesn't have to be the entire wing of a hospital, but should have enough supplies to cover most mishaps.

8. Flashlight. For those outings when you don't quite make it back to the car before sunset.

9. Map. On longer hikes and overnight trips, such as Big Lake Wilderness or Isle Royale National Park, a guidebook can never replace a good map.

10. Compass. A map is of little use unless you have a compass and the ability to orient yourself.

■ SAFETY

We all want to enter the woods and come out . . . safely. Hiking, canoeing, skiing, and all other forms of backcountry travel entail a certain amount of risk, especially when children are involved. No guidebook, no matter how well researched and written, can alert you to every hazard or anticipate your abilities and limitations. In the end, you alone are responsible for your own safety and that of those in your party.

But risks can be minimized and most mishaps avoided if you are prepared before you head out, and alert once you are on the trail. Be conscious of your drinking water. The best bet is to carry a water bottle and not depend on any untested source to quench a thirst. Regardless of whether it is from Lake Superior or a small trout stream, all water in Michigan should be considered affected by *Giardia lamblia* (an intestinal parasite). If you do need to use water from a lake or river, either boil it for one full minute or run it through one of several filters on the market today, which are designed to remove the parasite.

You should also be aware of the hazards of hypothermia and its symptoms, even during summer trips. Because of their small body size, children are more vulnerable to exposure and a drop in the body's internal temperature than adults. A child with the first stages of hypothermia is often listless, unwilling to cooperate, and whiny. Then the common physical signs, such as uncontrolled shivering, set in. Be alert to any of these signs and work quickly to rewarm the young hiker with food, hot drink, additional clothing, or an extended break in a sleeping bag.

Less threatening are sore feet and bug bites, but they can ruin a trip just as easily. It is best to solve potential foot problems before the hike by selecting the proper boots or tennis shoes and then making sure they fit and are broken in. But always carry a supply of moleskin and bandages for when a blister suddenly develops two miles from the trailhead.

Also pack insect repellents, as well as long-sleeve shirts, pants, and hats during the summer to combat mosquitoes, no-see-ums, deerflies, and blackflies. Most important, on overnight trips have a tent with insect screening that has been double-checked for even the tiniest hole. You can survive bugs during the day as long as you have a safe haven to escape from them at night.

■ TEACHING OUTDOOR ETHICS

Children emulate their parents. If you have a genuine love for the outdoors, it doesn't take long for them to begin enjoying day hikes, camping trips, or a backpacking adventure into any of Michigan's many wilderness areas. If you show a fear of bears, snakes, or other wildlife, your children will soon come to detest those animals as well. All this should be kept in mind when you're heading outdoors, for what you teach and display in the first few years will set a pattern for the rest of your children's lives.

I loathe trash on the trail or a beer bottle in the river, and it wasn't long before my daughter said the only thing worse than a biting deerfly was a litterbug. By age five she was pouncing on trash left lying in the middle of a campsite and teaching her younger brother to do the same.

Show them how to leave a backcountry campsite as though it had never been there to begin with. Teach them not to litter, disfigure campground facilities, or bathe in a lake. Explain to them that the most beautiful trees are the ones without names, hearts, or arrows carved in the bark. Tell them that everything you pack in, you pack out, because there are no "trash days" in the wilderness.

Help them to see the beauty of wildlife and thus develop a respect for the other animals that share the woods. Lead them to a quiet stand of hardwoods, a world without man-made noise, and then sit back while they hear their first leaf fall. Spend a moment on a trout stream, where the water is so clear and unpolluted, you can watch mayflies hatch on the surface or fish dart below.

Such simple discoveries now will make for permanent judgments later. Who knows? A child's walk in the woods while holding dad's hand may be just enough to save a forest in the future.

Opposite: *Young hikers look for aquatic wildlife, Graham Lakes Loop*

SOUTHEAST MICHIGAN

1.
WALK-IN-THE-WATER
CANOE TRAIL
OAKWOODS METROPARK

Activities: Canoeing, interpretive center, scenic cruise
County: Wayne
Difficulty: Easy
Length: 1-mile loop
Fee: Vehicle entry fee
Information: Oakwoods Metropark nature center, (313) 782-3956 or 1-800-24-PARKS

■ The old oxbows, marshes, and backwater bayous of the lower Huron River enable Oakwoods Metropark to offer a most unusual "nature trail"—you follow this one in a canoe, not on foot. Named Walk-in-the-Water after a prominent

Paddler enjoying the Walk-in-the-Water Canoe Trail, Oakwoods Metropark

Wyandotte Indian chief, the self-guiding canoe trail is a 1-mile loop through the flat and calm waters created by the Flat Rock Dam. Park officials claim this is the only canoe trail in Michigan and one of the few in the country today.

Maybe there should be more. This is an excellent choice for a child's first canoeing experience. The paddling is easy, the lily pads, cattails, and other marsh plants interesting, and the wildlife, such as turtles, waterfowl, and muskrats, intriguing to children. Best of all, even without someone paddling consistently in the front, the loop takes only about an hour—just the right length for a child's first canoe trip.

The park is located in the southeast corner of Wayne County and is reached from I-275 by departing west onto South Huron Drive (exit 11) and then immediately turning south onto Bell Road. Follow the paved and dirt road for 1.5 miles and then turn east (left) onto Willow Road for 1 mile to the posted entrance. It's a 2-mile drive along the park road to the parking lot and nature center.

A visit to the center is a good introduction to the trail. There are exhibits of live animals—snakes, turtles, and aquariums full of fish—as well as several excellent hands-on displays. One, "Making Tracks," has children use large rubber discs to leave the prints of ten different animals in the sand while "Nature Scents" has them guessing what the smell is (wild peppermint, of course). The center is open from 10:00 A.M. to 5:00 P.M. daily in the summer. During the school year the hours change to 1:00 to 5:00 P.M. weekdays and 10:00 A.M. to 5:00 P.M. weekends.

They don't rent canoes at Oakwoods, but they do have "The Huron," a 34-foot-long replica of the canoes used by the "voyageurs," the French Canadian adventurers and fur traders who frequented the Great Lakes during the nineteenth century. The boat holds eighteen people and is used for naturalist-led tours of the canoe trail. The trips last an hour and are offered throughout the summer and on weekends during autumn, by far the best time to visit this interesting stretch of the Huron River because of the outstanding fall colors that peak at the end of October.

A trip on the voyageurs canoe is a unique cruise, but paddling a boat on your own is the best way to experience the river trail. You can launch your boat from a dock near the nature center and travel in a counterclockwise direction past the many lily-pad-covered channels and marshy islets along this loop. Eight interpretive stops, almost within sight of each other, are strung along the route. Each of the floating bleach bottle markers has a nature lesson attached underneath. Pick the bottles up and read aloud to learn about cattails, birds that frequent this area, or how an oxbow is formed.

Pushing off from the dock, you'll first paddle with the current, passing the center's river observation platform on the right bank. Curve north and west 180 degrees past a small island with a huge willow tree and begin heading upstream. The current is never threatening and the water rarely deep, even when you're paddling through the swiftest water formed by the narrow gap at the logjam. Just before that section is the entrance to Middlebelt Bayou, which can be an extension to the trip and a chance either to view the waterfowl

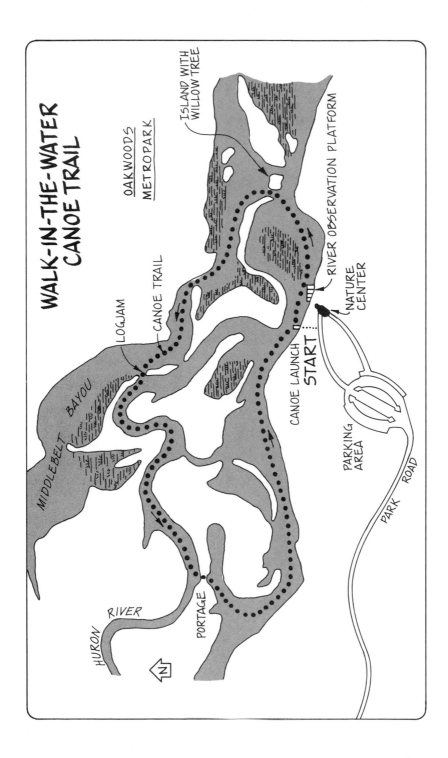

WALK-IN-THE-WATER
CANOE TRAIL

OAKWOODS
METROPARK

ISLAND WITH
WILLOW TREE

RIVER OBSERVATION PLATFORM

NATURE
CENTER

CANOE TRAIL

LOGJAM

MIDDLEBELT BAYOU

CANOE LAUNCH

START

PARKING
AREA

PARK ROAD

HURON RIVER

PORTAGE

N

and birdlife that often gather there or to put the lines out in an effort to catch crappie or other panfish, or even smallmouth bass.

Beyond the logjam the channel is narrow until you reach the posted portage, a quick walk around another logjam in the river. On the other side you return to paddling with the slow current. The dock will come into view in a few minutes, but before it does, keep an eye on the floating logs and deadheads here. If the sun is out, turtles will be everywhere, basking in the warmth and providing many children their first opportunity to observe wildlife in its natural state.

Shhhh! Let's see how close we can get to the log.

2.
MAYBURY
LIVING FARM
MAYBURY STATE PARK

Activities: Bicycling, interpretive center, skiing
County: Wayne
Difficulty: Moderate
Length: 4- to 5-mile loop
Fee: Vehicle entry fee
Information: Park headquarters, (313) 349-8390

In the corner of Wayne County, on the edge of metropolitan Detroit but worlds away, are rolling wooded hills, a fishing pond, and even a working farm. Maybury State Park, a 946-acre unit established in 1975, is a good destination for a variety of outdoor adventures for children. Most of the park is inaccessible to vehicles and can be enjoyed only on foot, skis, horseback, or—perhaps the best way—on bicycle.

Pack a lunch and a fishing rod, and then plan to ride from the bicycle concession building out to the pond and back again, a 4- to 5-mile trip that can include numerous stops. The paved paths are well marked and pass numerous covered benches in case it starts sprinkling. About the only thing that will slow up a young rider are a few uphill

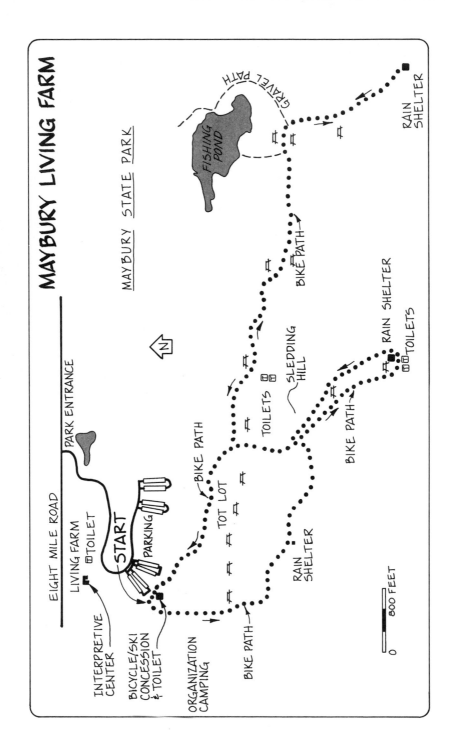

MAYBURY LIVING FARM

MAYBURY STATE PARK

EIGHT MILE ROAD

PARK ENTRANCE

LIVING FARM ⊞TOILET

START

PARKING

INTERPRETIVE CENTER

BICYCLE/SKI CONCESSION & TOILET

ORGANIZATION CAMPING

BIKE PATH

TOT LOT

BIKE PATH

RAIN SHELTER

TOILETS

SLEDDING HILL

BIKE PATH

BIKE PATH

RAIN SHELTER

RAIN SHELTER ⊞⊞TOILETS

FISHING POND

GRAVEL PATH

RAIN SHELTER

N

0 — 800 FEET

The tot lot along the bicycle path, Maybury State Park

stretches. It surprises most people that Wayne County can be this hilly.

The park is reached from I-275 by departing at Eight Mile Road (exit 167) and heading west for 5 miles. To reach the headquarters or riding stable within the park, head south 0.25 mile from Eight Mile Road on Beck Road. To reach the main entrance into Maybury, continue on Eight Mile Road. Near the parking area is the bicycle concession (313-348-1190), open on weekends in spring and fall.

Nearby is Maybury Living Farm, an area of several barns, many pens, and a lot of farm machinery. The park staff actually works the 40-acre farm and encourages children and families to wander through the barns, feed the animals, or watch huge draft horses pull a plow through a field of corn or oats. Animals range from cows and pigs to goats, chickens, sheep, and other typical farm stock. The interpretive center (313-349-0817) is open daily from 10:00 A.M. to 7:00 P.M. Labor Day to Memorial Day and 10:00 A.M. to 5:00 P.M. the rest of the year.

You can pick up the bicycle path from several points, including in front of the concession building. Head south on the path, quickly passing the entrance to the park's organization campground and then entering the woods where there are picnic tables, grills, and a posted path to the tot lot. The next 0.5 mile is in the woods as the path curves east, passing a covered bench along the way and ending at a somewhat confusing junction. If you turn south, you'll enter a 0.75-mile loop that passes two picnic areas, the second being one of the most scenic in the park. The tables are set up under a stand of pine trees at the top of a low hill in a quiet back section of the park.

Just north of the loop is a second junction, this one with a bike path leading to the east side of the park. The 1.5-mile, one-way ride ends at a covered bench in the southeast corner after passing over several hills. The terrain changes from pleasant stands of forest to an open hillside, and along the way you pass a picnic shelter, the steep sledding hill, and 1 mile from the junction the posted path to the fishing pond. It's less than a 0.2-mile walk to the large pond with its docks and fishing pier, where it is possible at times to catch panfish or even bass.

Back at the second junction, the main loop curves northwest, coming quickly to the park's central picnic area. An older forest rings an open picnic area that includes two shelters, toilets, water pump, tables, grills, and the impressive tot lot, a play area of eight wooden structures that seem to blend in with the surrounding trees. From the play area the path continues through the forest for 0.3 mile until you end back at the bicycle concession.

WINTER USE

From early January through February, you can combine a ski trip with a farm visit at Maybury. The bicycle concession becomes a cross-country ski rental and warming center, open noon to 6:00 P.M. Monday through Friday and 9:00 A.M. to

6:00 P.M. Saturday and Sunday. Call the bicycle concession phone number for snow conditions. The sledding and toboggan hill is a 0.7-mile walk from the east parking area and situated nearby is a partially enclosed shelter with a fireplace.

3.
WILDWING
LAKE
KENSINGTON METROPARK

Activities: Day hike, interpretive center
County: Livingston and Oakland
Difficulty: Easy
Length: 2.2-mile loop
Fee: Vehicle entry fee
Information: Park headquarters, (313) 685-1561 or 1-800-24-PARKS

■ Kensington Metropark can be a zoo at times—for the wrong reasons. On a holiday weekend, it's overflowing with joggers, boaters, and family get-togethers. But even then you can find areas within the 4,337-acre park to escape the crowds and heat, stroll along a shaded forest trail, and view a variety of wildlife. In the northwest corner of the park is Kensington's nature study area, featuring an interpretive center, several ponds and lakes, and more than 7 miles of foot trails, including one that skirts the edge of Wildwing Lake.

The Wildwing trail is an easy 2.2-mile hike that can be accomplished in tennis shoes. Along it you'll spot a variety of wildlife, from chipmunks to whistling swans and other waterfowl, to any of the 100 white-tailed deer estimated to be living in the park. Wildwing is marked by more than a dozen interpretive plaques explaining such subjects as dying lakes, glaciers, and the importance of wetlands. When combined with a visit to the nature center, the hike makes for an educational experience as well as a short outdoor adventure for children. If this path is too long, there are three other posted trails—

Tamarack, Deer Run, and Aspen—which range from 0.5 to 1.8 miles.

The park straddles the Oakland-Livingston county border and can be reached from I-96 by departing at Kensington Road (exit 151) or Kent Lake Road (exit 153), just east of US-23. Head north on either and signs will direct you to the park entrance and the nature center. The nature study area has its own parking area and on the way to the interpretive building you pass Kingfisher Lagoon and its carp pond on the west end. The huge fish can be seen lazily swimming during the summer and an interpretive plaque explains their arrival in the United States. The nature center contains an exhibit room with an active beehive, freshwater aquariums, exhibits of other cold-blooded animals, and several hands-on displays, including "touch test boxes." During the summer the building is open 10:00 A.M. to 5:00 P.M. daily; the rest of the year, hours are 1:00 to 5:00 P.M. weekdays and 10:00 A.M. to 5:00 P.M. weekends.

All trails depart from the center and along the Wildwing you quickly come to a junction with the Aspen Trail and the rock viewing area, where an interpretive display shows and explains the differences between metamorphic, sedimentary, and igneous rocks. The trail passes through a field of cattails and in 0.4 mile reaches another access point to the Aspen Trail and a rest area with covered benches and a hand pump for water. The wide, wood-chip path soon becomes a narrow forest trail, reaching the first bridge in 0.5 mile and the overlook 1 mile from the beginning. Keep an eye out for the tree identification signs 12 feet up the trunks, explaining the characteristics of white pine, basswood, trembling aspen, and other species.

At the overlook are a pair of benches and a view of the lake. Saplings partially block the view now, so some children might have to climb onto dad's or mom's shoulders to see the water. The trail descends immediately after the overlook and swings around the southwest corner of the lake, breaking out near the park road at one point. But that is only a brief intrusion, and the path quickly swings away from the cars and

Swans in Wildwing Lake, Kensington Metropark

pavement to stay close to the shoreline. Almost every step along this section offers a view of the lake, and in midsummer the hundreds of greater white lily flowers are dazzling. So are the resident swans—huge birds that will immediately let a youngster know when he or she has ventured too close.

The second bridge is reached 1.8 miles from the beginning, at which point the trail briefly follows the park road, providing a view of Kent Lake to the east. You end on a service drive back at the rock display area.

4. HURON SWAMP
INDIAN SPRINGS METROPARK

Activities: Bicycling, interpretive center, day hike, skiing
County: Oakland
Difficulty: Moderate
Length: 8 miles round-trip
Fee: Vehicle entry fee
Information: Indian Springs Metropark nature center, (313) 625-7280 or 1-800-24-PARKS

Many children have negative images of wetlands. Rarely have they explored one and most of their knowledge comes from second-rate Japanese movies that show lizardlike men emerging from swamps and bogs to terrorize the countryside. Unfortunately, some kids grow up never experiencing the wildlife and beauty wetlands offer, nor understanding the value of them.

Indian Springs Metropark in northwest Oakland County offers not only a nature center where children can learn about wetlands but also an opportunity to see one firsthand, either by bicycle or on foot. The park was established in 1982 to preserve the last major section of the Huron Swamp and features 6 miles of nature trails and 5 miles of paved bicycle path. Meadowlark Picnic Area has tables, grills, shelters, and toilets, but the park has no facilities for camping or swimming.

The park can be reached from M-24 (Dixie Highway) in Clarkston by heading west on White Lake Road and following it 5 miles to the posted entrance. It can also be reached from M-59 by turning north on Ormond Road and then east on White Lake Road. The park is open daily from 8:00 A.M. to dusk; the nature center's hours are 10:00 A.M. to 5:00 P.M. daily from June 15 to September 14. During the rest of the year the building is open 1:00 to 5:00 P.M. on weekdays and 10:00 A.M. to 5:00 P.M. on Saturday and Sunday.

The nature center is an attractive building that uses solar energy for heat and has natural lighting. Along with bathrooms, lounge, and a classroom, there is an interesting exhibit area devoted to wetlands. One display, entitled "The Huron River from Ice to Erie," traces the history of the river and diagrams its 115-mile route from its mouth in Lake Erie to its headwaters, the Huron Swamp that lies just outside.

There are also exhibits on birdlife of the area; the differences between bogs, marshes, and swamps; live reptiles and amphibians; and, perhaps the most interesting display for children, the "pond critters" table. The table is a waist-high, shallow pool filled with the thriving life of a swamp: tadpoles, leeches, caddis flies, even frogs with tails that have yet to disappear. By looking at, listening to, and touching the animals, children learn that swamps are not just mud and water.

Then you can head outside and show them the real thing. Just outside the center is the trailhead for the Woodland Trail, a 2-mile walk through a swamp land of towering trees, with two crossings of the Huron River, just a slow-moving creek at this point. Or you can view portions of the Huron Swamp by pedaling perhaps the only Michigan bicycle path through a wetland.

Because this is a wetland, the best time of year for the adventure is either late spring, when there is a profusion of wildflowers, or in the fall, when the leaves of the maple and oak that forest much of the area turn. During late June and early July, Indian Springs usually has more than its share of mosquitoes and deerflies. The paved path makes for an 8-mile round-trip, beginning at Meadowlark Picnic Area. The first mile parallels the park road through open fields and descends a steep hill before crossing the creek that is the Huron River.

At this point the path swings sharply to the north and enters the woods. Even if they never leave the bike trail (who wants mud on their shoes?), children can peer through the trees to view the wet ground and an occasional stagnant pond—characteristics of a swamp. In late spring and early summer, flowers, such as wood lilies, black-eyed Susans, and woodland sunflowers, add a dash of color to the ride. Both the kilometers and the miles have been marked on the path and just before reaching the 3-mile point, you pass the largest ponds, as well as some large open fields that were once farmed.

At 3 miles is a junction in the trail, along with a rest area that has toilets, a hand pump for water, and a picnic table. Go either direction on the 2-mile loop through woods and open fields before returning to the rest area, where you will backtrack to Meadowlark Picnic Area. Keep in mind that the hill everybody went flying down at the beginning is now a long uphill climb, especially for the short legs of six- and seven-year-old cyclists. Luckily, at the top, under a large shade tree, is a bench where you can rest and enjoy a pleasant overview of the Huron River flowing south out of the park.

WINTER USE

When there is sufficient snow, usually January through February, park trails are groomed for cross-country skiing. A ski rental is operated out of the nature center and skiers use the lounge with its wood-burning stove as a warming area.

5.
PAINT
CREEK
PAINT CREEK TRAIL

Activities: Day hike, interpretive center
County: Oakland
Difficulty: Moderate
Length: 2.4 miles one way
Fee: None
Information: Dinosaur Hill Nature Center, (313) 656-0999

■ Some people find it hard to believe that within the rapid development of Oakland County, one of the fastest-growing areas of Michigan, a 9-mile trail that for the most part is a wooded path winds along a trout stream. Paint Creek Trail, which runs from Clinton River south of Rochester to Lake Orion, was the first rails-trails project to be completed in the state. Leftover rail-roading artifacts from the Penn Central Line, including rails, wood ties, even communication boxes, still litter the area, but now the raised bed is an avenue of escape from the boom and construction of northern Detroit.

The entire trail makes for a long day, too long for most children, but one stretch lies between a nature center in Rochester and a cider mill north, ideal places to begin and end an afternoon outing. This 2.4-mile hike is along the trail's most scenic section, where it frequently crosses Paint Creek, a stream stocked annually with trout. The wide, level path is most spectacular during the fall colors of October, when you can view the autumn reds and oranges of hardwoods and then end the walk with a jug of freshly squeezed apple cider.

Dinosaur Hill Nature Center, named after a hill that children said looked like a sleeping dinosaur, is located on the northern edge of Rochester and is bordered on one side by Paint Creek. The 16-acre preserve is reached from Rochester Road (Main Street in town) by turning west onto Woodward for two blocks and then north on Oak Street to North

PAINT CREEK TRAIL

PAINT CREEK

PAINT

GALLAGHER RD.

PAINT CREEK
CIDER MILL

SILVER BELL
ROAD

ORION CREEK

DUTTON ROAD

ROAD

TIENKEN ROAD

DINOSAUR HILL
NATURE CENTER

TRAIL

ROCHESTER
START

N

0   1 MILE

Hill Circle, where the entrance is posted to the west. Dinosaur Hill includes an interpretive center, three self-guided nature trails, and quick access to Paint Creek. Hours are 9:00 A.M. to 2:00 P.M. Monday through Thursday, and 10:00 A.M. to 1:00 P.M. weekends.

One of the nature paths leads to Paint Creek Trail, which heads north on the west bank of the river. You immediately come to Tienken Road and on the north side cross a bridge over the creek. There are houses within view of the trail at first, but gradually you leave the sights and sounds of Rochester behind to wander through the woods with the trout stream gurgling beside you. This is greater metropolitan Detroit? Amazing. Within a mile of the nature center you

Family closely examining Paint Creek along the Paint Creek Trail

cross the creek a second time and pass a series of steps leading down to the water—good place for a break.

Two more bridges are crossed, one on each side of Dutton Road, and from the second some members of your hiking party might be tempted by a long rope swing tied to a tree leaning over a deep pool in Paint Creek. A few more bridges and 2 miles from the nature center, the trail approaches Silver Bell Road. Just before the road, the banks of the creek have been reinforced with logs, the work of a local Trout Unlimited Chapter. Logs and rocks have been used to stabilize eroding portions of the stream, which were making the water too silty for trout eggs to hatch. Natural reproduction now occurs and, combined with annual plantings, makes Paint Creek a popular destination for anglers who bait small hooks with worms and occasionally pull out rainbow trout up to 15 inches in length.

On the north side of Silver Bell Road, the trail becomes a wide, gravel path that parallels the creek. The stream swings close to the path several times and 2.2 miles from the start you come to another set of steps that overlook an S-bend in the creek. It's a scenic spot to sit and whittle the afternoon away, especially if you brought a pole and a can of worms along. If it's July, tell the troops to keep an eye out for wild raspberries, which grow along this stretch of the trail. A ripe berry is a real find, however. Between the abundance of birds in the area and passing hikers, few berries hang on the bush for very long.

Just before reaching Gallagher Road, you see the backside of Paint Creek Cider Mill along the stream. The historic mill is located on the corner of Gallagher and Orion Road in the community of Goodison. From September through Christmas the mill makes apple cider and is open from 9:00 A.M. to 6:00 P.M. daily. During the summer it switches to selling ice cream and is open 11:00 A.M. to 8:00 P.M. Tuesday through Saturday and until 6:00 P.M. on Sunday. For children, either treat is welcome after conquering Paint Creek Trail.

6.
GRAHAM
LAKES
BALD MOUNTAIN RECREATION AREA

Activity: Day hike
County: Oakland
Difficulty: Moderate
Length: 3.6-mile loop
Fee: Vehicle entry fee
Information: Park headquarters, (313) 693-6767

█ Northern Oakland County can be a surprisingly rugged area and the best example of this is Bald Mountain Recreation Area. There is no actual "Bald Mountain" in the state recreation area, but the trail system in the park's northern unit does climb and descend a number of ridges and hills, and to young hikers these are mountains indeed. The 8-mile network is composed of three main loops and is most popular among cross-country skiers, who like the challenge of the hilly terrain.

But during the summer the Graham Lakes Loop, a 3.6-mile walk, makes one of the better day hikes for children in the metropolitan Detroit area. The adventure includes good ridgetop views, along with almost a dozen lakes and ponds in the lowlands, where such wildlife as grouse, cottontail rabbits, Canada geese, and possibly even a deer can be spotted. Come spring the patches of wildflowers around the wetlands are extensive, and in the autumn the ponds are highlighted by fall colors of hardwood trees. Summer is nice, too, but remember that these stagnant bodies of water are natural hatcheries for mosquitoes, especially late May through June.

The northern unit of the recreation area is located east of Lake Orion and can be reached from M-24 by following Clarkston Road, an especially scenic route where it forms an S-turn to cross Paint Creek. After 2 miles turn north on Adams Road, which ends at Stoney Creek Road. Head east 100 yards and then north on Harmon Road, which leads into the

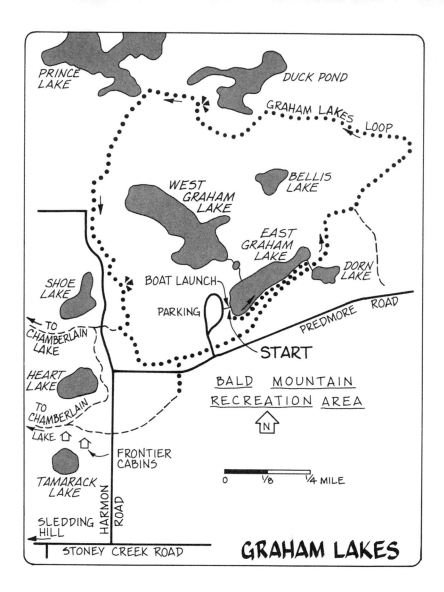

PRINCE LAKE

DUCK POND

GRAHAM LAKES LOOP

BELLIS LAKE

WEST GRAHAM LAKE

EAST GRAHAM LAKE

DORN LAKE

SHOE LAKE

BOAT LAUNCH

PARKING

TO CHAMBERLAIN LAKE

PREDMORE ROAD

START

HEART LAKE

TO CHAMBERLAIN LAKE

BALD MOUNTAIN RECREATION AREA

FRONTIER CABINS

0   1/8   1/4 MILE

TAMARACK LAKE

HARMON ROAD

SLEDDING HILL

STONEY CREEK ROAD

GRAHAM LAKES

park. There are four trailheads and parking areas for the Graham Lakes Loop, including one at the end of Harmon Road.

A nice way to hike this trail is to begin at the East Graham Lake boat launch, which is reached by turning onto Predmore Road from Harmon and heading east for a quarter mile. By starting here and walking counterclockwise, you put the heavily forested stretch in the middle of the hike and save the best view for the end.

A large wooden display sign marks the trail and hikers should head east from there. Within 0.5 mile you follow the south shore of East Graham Lake and then cross a wooden bridge over the stream that connects East Graham to Dorn Lake. The trail winds away from the lakes, passes a dozen impressive anthills, and then enters the forest. Now this is a hike. Within the next mile you climb up and over several hills, pass a handful of ponds, and rarely break out of the trees until you reach one arm of Duck Pond.

The best view of the large pond is in another 0.5 mile, or 1.9 miles from the boat launch, where you ascend to a bench with Duck Pond to the north and the surrounding hills to the west. The trail emerges from the trees again when you come to Prince Lake, roughly the halfway point and a logical lunch spot. Avoid the trails that wander around the lake and soon you'll enter a pine plantation whose towering trees are in perfect rows. In the middle is another bench.

Within 0.6 mile from Prince Lake the trail leaves the trees to pass a private home and then arrive at the posted trailhead at the end of the Harmon Road. The trail heads south from here, crosses a wooden bridge over a stream, and then begins to ascend. Is this Bald Mountain? somebody is bound to ask. Well, no, but to young hikers it does seem like climbing a peak. On the way up you pass a view of Shoe Lake and then actually do "top out" at a clearing with a bench and a panorama of West Graham Lake and many of the surrounding ridges you've already walked over.

After a quick descent into open fields, you pass the posted junction to Chamberlain Lake, 0.5 mile from the Harmon Road trailhead. Swing east into the woods to emerge at the boat launch parking area within a few minutes.

7.
CROOKED
LAKE
INDEPENDENCE OAKS COUNTY PARK

Activities: Day hike, fishing, interpretive center, skiing
County: Oakland
Difficulty: Easy
Length: 2.4-mile loop
Fee: Vehicle entry fee
Information: Park office, (313) 625-0877

■ Independence Oaks is an 850-acre park featuring rolling hills, wooded ravines, the headwaters of the Clinton River, and a variety of wildlife including white-tailed deer. But the

Skier and her pulk, a sled designed to pull children, Independence Oaks County Park

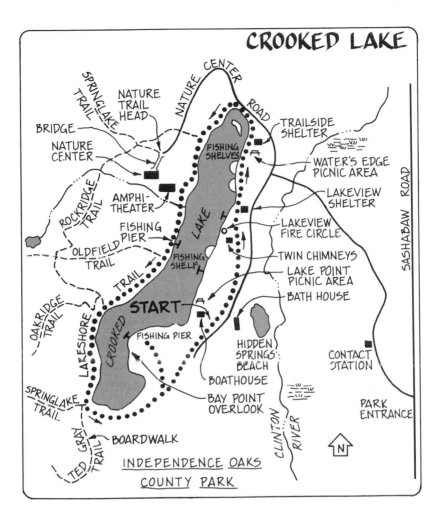

INDEPENDENCE OAKS
COUNTY PARK

centerpiece of this Oakland County Park is Crooked Lake, a 68-acre body of water with an undeveloped shoreline. Circling the lake is Lakeshore Trail, a 2.4-mile loop used by hikers in the summer and groomed and tracked for skiers in the winter.

The park has a 10-mile network of trails but Lakeshore is the ideal one for children, whether they are walking or skiing. It's not only an easy trip but also a scenic trek with a view of the lake almost every step of the way. The water, and the wildlife found in and on it, holds the interest of kids, keeping their minds off tired legs.

Independence Oaks is located north of the village of Clarkston and can be reached from I-75 by exiting at Sashabaw Road (exit 89). Head north for 2 miles to the posted entrance. The park also features picnic areas, several shelters, a swimming area on Hidden Spring, and a boathouse that rents out canoes, rowboats, and pedal boats, and sells bait during the summer.

The boathouse, with its indoor bathrooms and refreshment counter, is the logical place to start the Lakeshore loop. Heading north, you skirt the lake's east side and pass its picnic areas and shelters. You also pass the first of several fishing docks with the third one situated over a drop-off in the lake, making it the best place to fish for panfish. The trail descends a small hill, rounding the north end of the lake and, once on the west side, comes to the junction with the Rockridge Trail. Follow Rockridge a short way to reach the park's nature center, which houses an exhibit room, a children's discovery corner, and a viewing window of its outdoor feeding station. The center is open daily 10:00 A.M. to 6:00 P.M. Memorial Day to Labor Day, and Tuesday through Sunday 10:00 A.M. to 5:00 P.M. the rest of the year.

The Lakeshore Trail continues following the west shore, passing first the shoreline picnic tables that mark the halfway point of the journey and then a small fishing dock. From the dock children can often watch a resident flock of mallards of Canada geese using the lake surface like a runway. If it's late April or May, have them search the crystal clear water for the sandy craters of spawning bluegill or other panfish. Find one of these underwater "dishes" and usually the protective mother is nearby.

If it's mid- to late summer take a rod and reel along and try fishing for panfish here or at one of the other docks the trail passes. Use a simple bobber rig with a leaf worm or half of a nightcrawler, which can be purchased from the boathouse. Young anglers rarely will catch a "keeper" off the docks, but the action is lively and often the highlight of a hike for children.

After the return junction of Rockridge Trail, the Lakeshore loop comes to its steepest drop before merging with the Springlake Trail at the south end of the lake. From here you are less than 0.5 mile from the boathouse, but don't pass up the side trail to Bay Point Overlook. This is an extremely pleasant spot with several picnic tables, another dock, and a nice view of the south end of the lake. Children will scamper down to the dock, where they can peer into the water and see snails, small fish, and other aquatic life. The final portion is along a service road through a moist and heavily wooded area where from April to early June wildflowers bloom in large gatherings.

WINTER USE

In the winter, the boathouse becomes a ski rental shop and warming center on the weekends from 8:00 A.M. until dusk. Lakeshore Trail becomes a novice ski run with only one low hill, near the return junction of Rockridge Trail at the south end of the lake, to befuddle a young skier. More advanced skiers can undertake the Rockridge Trail, rated intermediate, or the 3.2-mile Springlake Trail, which offers some of the steepest hills for nordic skiers in Oakland County.

8.
ROSTON
CABIN
HOLLY RECREATION AREA

Activities: Frontier cabin, skiing
County: Oakland
Difficulty: Easy
Fee: Vehicle entry fee, cabin rental fee
Information: Park headquarters, (313) 634-8811

■ Winter camping made easy? Well, maybe not easy, but Roston Cabin in Holly Recreation Area makes a weekend spent in the winter woods as comfortable and warm as sitting around a fireplace at night or stoking up the wood-burning stove before breakfast. The cabin is snug and tight, yet rustic and secluded enough to make it seem like an adventure in the woods, even with the car parked right outside.

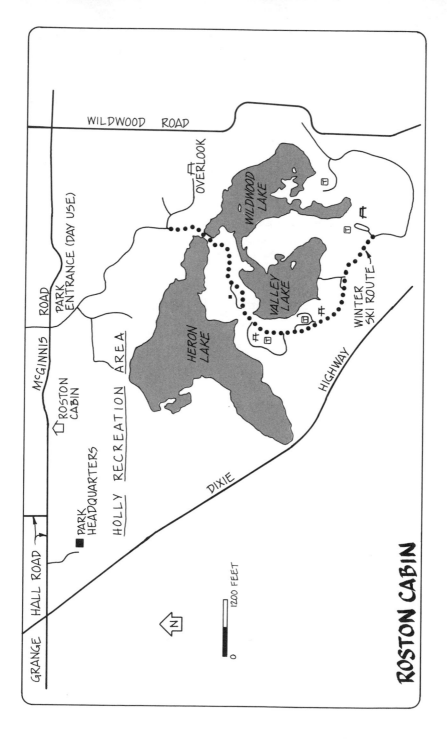

ROSTON CABIN

WILDWOOD ROAD

OVERLOOK

WILDWOOD LAKE

VALLEY LAKE

WINTER SKI ROUTE

HERON LAKE

PARK ENTRANCE (DAY USE)

ROAD

McGINNIS

ROSTON CABIN

HOLLY RECREATION AREA

PARK HEADQUARTERS

HIGHWAY

DIXIE

GRANGE HALL ROAD

N

1200 FEET

0

You can rent this frontier cabin year-round, but from late December through February, children will discover the quiet and very white world of a state park during the off-season. Reach the cabin by departing I-75 east onto Grange Hall Road (exit 101) and following it east past Dixie Highway. The posted park headquarters is just beyond on the south (right) side of the road and then Grange Hall Road takes a sharp curve north. But park signs direct you straight onto McGinnis Road where you'll quickly come to the dirt drive and locked gate of the cabin on the south side of the road.

It's necessary to reserve the cabin in advance, several months if possible, by calling the park headquarters. If you plan to arrive during the winter, bring warm sleeping bags, heavy clothing, boots, parkas, cooking utensils, pans, and food.

Built by the Roston family as a weekend cottage in the early 1940s, the structure was later obtained by the park, which began renting it out in 1984. This classic cabin, with walls of logs, polished planked floors, and red-checkered curtains on the windows, is located between a small pond (full of frogs during the summer) and a cattail marsh (where deer often wander through at dusk). There is electricity and the kitchen features a stove and refrigerator, as well as a table, benches, and a wood-burning stove. The sleeping room is larger, with a set of bunks and an easy chair facing a field-stone fireplace. Overlooking the cozy room is a loft with four more mattresses. Outside you'll find a vault toilet, woodshed, a hand pump for water, and a barbecue grill.

WINTER USE

By far the favorite activity of winter renters is cross-country skiing. Follow McGinnis Road another 0.25 mile east to the entrance of Heron Lake day-use area. The scenic road winds 3 miles south around three lakes, Heron, Valley, and Wildwood, but isn't plowed much beyond Overlook picnic area. At this point the road becomes a perfect ski run through the rolling terrain of meadows and woods, providing views of the lakes much of the way.

9.
HURON
RIVER
ISLAND LAKE STATE RECREATION AREA

Activities: Canoeing, camping
County: Livingston
Difficulty: Moderate
Length: 8.5 miles one way
Fee: Vehicle entry fee, camping fee
Information: Park headquarters, (313) 229-7067

■ Many canoeists think southern Michigan is lucky to have the Huron River. Within a 90-minute drive of one of the largest cities in the country is a waterway so undeveloped that it has been designated a Country Scenic National River. The

Above: Angling for bass, Yankee Springs Recreation

entire river is a 100-mile paddle from Proud Lake to the Pointe Mouillee State Game Area near its mouth on Lake Erie. But the most scenic stretch is also the best one for children and can be handled as a day paddle or turned into a unique overnight adventure in the middle of the woods, something that's hard to do this close to Detroit.

The 8.5-mile stretch from the Kent Lake Dam to US-23 splits Island Lake State Recreation Area in half and for the most part is a 40- to 60-foot-wide river with a slow-moving current. A few fallen trees must be negotiated and it's possible a sweeper might force paddlers out of the boat at low water, but there are no rapids, not even a threatening ripple. The entire route could be paddled by an adult and child in 4 to 5 hours, but a canoe campground, which is accessible only by the river, is strategically located in the middle of the park. You can paddle 2 hours one day, camp overnight along the riverbank, and then finish up the outing with a 2-hour paddle the next morning and a child who is as enthusiastic about canoeing at the end as he or she was in the beginning. This is an especially good trip for September or October, since much of the river winds through a forest of maple, oak, and ask.

The state park is reached from I-96 by departing south onto Kensington Road (exit 151). The park headquarters is posted and will provide either a "Huron River Canoeing Map," put out by the Huron-Clinton Metropolitan Authority, or, even better, a park map. The put-in is the day-use area on Kent Lake, with an entrance drive just south of park headquarters on Kensington Road. Near the west end of the lake is Heavner Canoe Livery (313-685-2379), which runs a rental concession in the park during the summer from noon to 6:00 P.M. daily. Renting a canoe with a scheduled pick-up solves the problem of returning to your vehicle; otherwise, another car can be left at the car pool parking area at the corner of Silver Lake and Fieldcrest roads just off US-23.

Begin by descending the log steps alongside Kent Lake Dam and launching the boat into the Huron River. The river begins as a wide and somewhat shallow waterway that flows over several stone walls and reaches the Kensington Road bridge in 20 to 30 minutes. No place to pull out here, but in another 20 minutes you arrive at a canoe access site with a

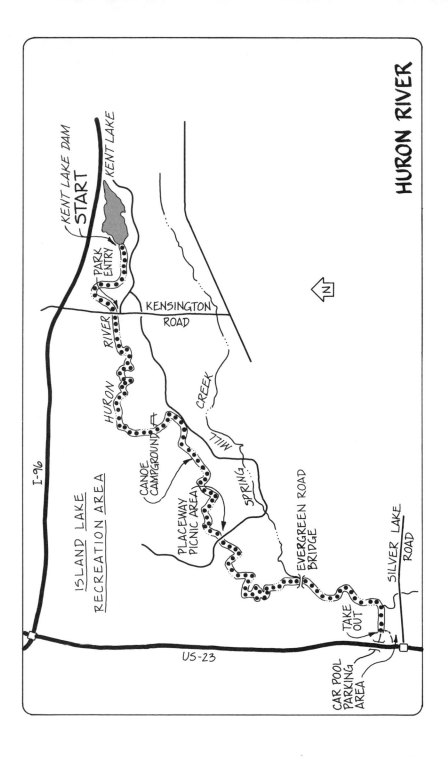

HURON RIVER

KENT LAKE DAM
START
KENT LAKE

PARK ENTRY

KENSINGTON ROAD

N

I-96

HURON RIVER

MILL CREEK

ISLAND LAKE
RECREATION AREA

CANOE CAMPGROUND

PLACEWAY PICNIC AREA

SPRING

EVERGREEN ROAD BRIDGE

SILVER LAKE ROAD

TAKE OUT

US-23

CAR POOL PARKING AREA

Campers at the canoe campground along the Huron River, Island Lake Recreation Area

picnic table and grill on a scenic bend of the river. The river flows through a marshlike terrain featuring rows of cattails and floating carpets of lily pads. Easy-to-spot turtles sun themselves on logs during the summer and on calm evenings fish rise to snatch hatching mayflies off the surface.

Eventually you pass some steep bluffs along the south bank and move into the forest for the first time, where some trees are so large they form a shaded arch above you. In 45 to 60 minutes from Kensington Road you pass a concrete bridge leading nowhere (the county road has been closed) and then reach the picnic tables, water pump, toilets, and shelter of Riverbend Picnic Area. From the day-use area, you quickly float under a railroad bridge and then reenter the shaded forest of towering trees—some actually touch each other over the water. Unfortunately, many have ended up in the river and occasionally the paddling gets tricky.

It takes only 15 to 20 minutes from the picnic area to reach the river signs that point out the two canoe campsites. Between them are pit toilets, a trash can, and a hand pump. Best to check the water situation before departing Kent Lake, because the pump is occasionally dry. The second site offers a particularly scenic spot to pitch a tent, with several picnic tables, a fire grill, and even a bench overlooking the river. No preregistration is needed to camp here, but at night a ranger passes through to collect a camping fee.

You continue through a wooded setting downstream from the campground and then begin a long float through a semiopen area where the river is bordered by grassy banks. Thirty minutes from the campground you reach Placeway Picnic Area, marked along the river by the sign "Bridge Picnic Area." The day-use area has tables, grills, and toilets and is located where State Park Drive crosses the Huron River. You float between forest and grassy banks and eventually leave the park, though you don't spot your first house until just before reaching Evergreen Road Bridge, where Spring Mill Creek empties into the river. From here it's another 40- to 50-minute paddle past an occasional house and around a number of fallen trees until you reach an obvious but unmarked take-out spot on the south banks of the river right before the US-23 bridge. A four-wheel track leads to the west (right) up a small hill to Fieldcrest Drive.

10.
POTAWATOMI
TRAIL
PINCKNEY RECREATION AREA

Activity: Backpacking
County: Livingston/Washtenaw
Difficulty: Challenging
Length: 11- to 17-mile loop
Fee: Vehicle entry fee, camping fee
Information: Park headquarters, (313) 426-4913

■ It's not the most scenic trail in Michigan. At times along the 17-mile Potawatomi Trail you'll see a private home here and there, or hear vehicles rumble by on a nearby road or motorboats on one of the many lakes in the Pinckney Recreation Area. But there also will be moments when the trail plunges into a thick oak forest, seemingly miles from any-where, passing small unnamed lakes without a soul on them or climbing to stunning overviews of this rugged region of the state.

Plus, there is the gratification all children feel when they emerge at the parking area that they left a day or two before.

The trail is well marked with mileposts and easy to fol-low. But there are few level stretches and following the entire route means a 10-mile trek the first day to the backpacker's campground on Blind Lake and a 7-mile return trip to the car on Silver Lake. The hike can be shortened, however, to 7 miles the first day and 4 miles the second, but either way this is an adventure too challenging for most children under the age of nine.

Fall is the prime time to hike the route because of the stands of oak and maple you pass through. Bring a lot of in-sect repellent during the summer and your own supply of water anytime of the year. The best place to pick up the trail is the Silver Lake day-use area reached from US-23 by de-parting west on North Territorial Road (exit 49) for 12 miles. Turn north (right) onto Dexter-Townhall Road for a mile to the posted entrance of the state recreation area on Silver Hill Road. The park headquarters is a half mile up the road where you register and pay for a night in the backpacker's campground. Just beyond are the parking lots for Silver Lake.

A large display map marks the trail at both the lower and upper parking areas, depending in which direction you are headed. By hiking in a counterclockwise direction and strik-ing out for Crooked Lake from the upper lot, you will be sav-ing the shorter and more scenic stretch for the second day. The trail begins by skirting Silver Lake, weaving between low-lying wet areas and young stands of trees. Within a half mile from the start, the trail swings west and begins a long as-cent away from the lake and into the woods. Two dirt roads are crossed and the first mile of the journey ends with an as-cent to a high point with an excellent view of Crooked Lake and the surrounding ridges.

This will give everybody in your party an idea of what kind of (up and down) hiking lies ahead.

The trail begins a long descent, bottoms out at a bridged

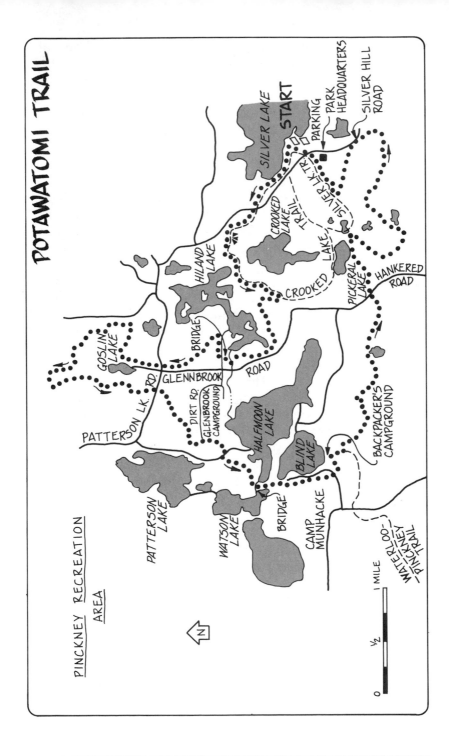

POTAWATOMI TRAIL

PINCKNEY RECREATION AREA

SILVER LAKE
START
PARKING
PARK HEADQUARTERS
SILVER HILL ROAD
SILVER LK. TR.
CROOKED LAKE TRAIL
CROOKED LAKE
CROOKED LAKE
PICKERAL LAKE
HANKERED ROAD
HILAND LAKE
GOSLIN LAKE
BRIDGE
GLENNBROOK ROAD
PATTERSON LK. RD.
DIRT RD.
GLENNBROOK CAMPGROUND
PATTERSON
HALFMOON LAKE
BLIND LAKE
BACKPACKER'S CAMPGROUND
PATTERSON LAKE
WATSON LAKE
BRIDGE
CAMP MUNHACKE
WATERLOO-PINCKNEY TRAIL

1 MILE
½
0

N

creek, and then climbs to a posted junction. Crooked Lake Trail departs south; you head north to swing past some marsh areas, two spurs to Glenbrook Road (stay to the right), and finally cross a huge wooden bridge over the channel between Halfmoon Lake and Hiland Lake at 3.4 miles. Just beyond that, you come to an unimproved road, where the trail continues on the other side, and then Patterson Lake Road at 4 miles. The unimproved road leads to Glenbrook Rustic Campground a half mile to the west, if you want to break the hike into three days. Patterson Road can be used to shorten the first half by almost 3 miles, as the trail recrosses the paved road 0.2 mile to the west.

To the north of Patterson Lake Road, the trail is a 3-mile loop that skirts Goslin Lake and continues to the edge of the state park (a towering fence marks the boundary) before swinging back south. On the other side of Patterson, the trail passes through some beautiful oak forests and even a stand of red pine before it begins a long descent to skirt around a marsh pond and then emerge at an unimproved road between Patterson and Halfmoon lakes at 8 miles. In another half mile you arrive at the large wooden bridge over the channel between Watson and Halfmoon lakes and then ascend to the most level stretch of the day through a semiopen area of scattered trees around Blind Lake.

The first day ends with you passing the posted junction to the Boy Scout Camp Munhacke, descending to an unimproved road, and emerging at an overgrown four-wheel drive track. A trail departs up the ridge here, but follow the track 0.5 mile to reach Blind Lake backpacker's campground. The grassy spot is on a small cove and makes for a scenic tent site. There is a vault toilet and trash barrel, but no water spigot or pump. You can pitch your tent a few feet from the lake and its small strip of sand.

The trail resumes near the vault toilet or you can backtrack to the spur that ascends the ridge. The spur climbs steeply up the ridge in a series of switchbacks but then gives way to one of the best views in the park. To the southwest you look over the rugged terrain of Waterloo Recreation Area and can see no less than ten forested ridges in different shades of green. From here you descend sharply to rejoin the

Potawatomi Trail at its junction with the Waterloo-Pinckney Trail.

To many this is the best stretch of the journey. The trail plunges into a thick hardwood forest and then climbs slightly to follow the crest of a narrow ridge. On both sides are steep drops to a ravine where a variety of wildlife—deer, raccoons, even flocks of wild turkeys—might be spotted. You skirt a small, roundish, unnamed lake 1.5 miles from the campground and then emerge at Hankered Road in another mile.

The trail resumes just to the south at the Pickeral Lake Access. It parallels the access road and then skirts the scenic lake from a high bank. Three miles from Blind Lake, you come to the well-posted junction with Silver Lake Trail. This path heads directly toward the Silver Lake parking area, which is reached in a mile. Potawatomi Trail heads southwest and weaves its way long the edge of numerous marsh areas and ponds before reaching the day-use area in 3.5 miles. The two trails merge as one for the final 0.5 mile before reaching the display map in the lower parking lot.

▌11.
BOG
TRAIL
WATERLOO RECREATION AREA

Activities: Day hike, interpretive center
County: Jackson
Difficulty: Easy
Length: Various lengths
Fee: Vehicle entry fee
Information: Gerald E. Eddy Geology Center, (313) 475-3170

■ Ask your children if they want to visit a nature center devoted to Michigan's geology and you'll probably receive a less than enthusiastic reply. But tell them it's a museum featuring crystals, fossils of prehistoric animals, even a collection of Indian arrowheads, and they'll be the first in the car for a trip to

Visitors study the wildlife displays, Gerald Eddy Geology Center, Waterloo Recreation Area

Gerald E. Eddy Geology Center, the newest state park interpretive center.

Located among the rolling hills of Waterloo Recreation Area, the center is between Jackson and Ann Arbor and reached from I-94 by departing north onto Pierce Road (exit 157) and then following brown park signs to the parking area. From there it's another quarter-mile walk along a paved path through the woods to the building.

The center features two main exhibit rooms, with the first devoted to Michigan's geological history. Displays explain the differences between igneous, metamorphic, and sedimentary rocks and describe each of the state's various geological eras. Much of this will be too complicated for children under the age of seven, but even they will enjoy peering through magnifying glasses at crystals, hunks of pure copper, and Petoskey stones and other fossils.

There are also murals depicting such scenes as Michigan buried under a glacier or when mastodons ruled the forests, the latter complete with a display case containing fossilized molars and ribs of the giant elephantlike animals. And everybody, regardless of age, is intrigued by the large collection of arrowheads.

The second exhibit room is devoted to the natural history of the state recreation area, with three-dimensional displays on the beaver, Waterloo's native Americans, and the variety of wildlife that might be seen along any trail in the park. Also featured are a collection of live turtles, displays on local birds, insects, and wildflowers, and a hands-on exhibit to help you identify the various species of trees in southeast Michigan.

All this new knowledge can be put to good use with a hike along one of the center's five trails. The longest is the Oakwoods Trail, an hour-long walk through an upland woods of oak and hickory. The 3-mile path runs along the base of several glacial hills and offers good views of Mill Lake.

But perhaps one of the most unique trails in southern Michigan is the center's floating bog walk. Plan on 20 to 30 minutes for the round-trip of 1.2 miles and first pick up the key at the center. The trail is marked along the paved entrance path and the locked gate is 0.3 mile from the trailhead.

Once through the gate, you enter a pleasant forest walk through a stand of large beech trees and then cross a boardwalk through a grove of ferns to reach the floating trail. The posted boardwalk extends out to a raft of unusual plants actually floating on an old lake. Children can reach down and push on the bog as if it were a water bed. Bring a plant book with you or study pictures in the interpretive center before departing to identify a variety of rare orchids or even insect-eating pitcher plants. Also bring insect repellent. This is, after all, a bog.

12. GRAVES HILL

YANKEE SPRINGS RECREATION AREA

Activity: Day hike
County: Barry
Difficulty: Easy to moderate
Length: 2- to 3-mile loop
Fee: Vehicle entry fee
Information: Park headquarters, (616) 795-9081

■ An old moraine makes a fine place for child's first "mountain climb" in southwest Michigan's Barry County. Graves Hill, the result of glacial activity, is located in the heart of Yankee Springs Recreation Area, one of the most popular units of the state park system. The loop trail is not strenuous but just steep enough to make children believe they're climbing a peak. The top rewards you with good views of the area, and the walk can be extended an extra mile to include Devils Soup Bowl, a deep depression.

Yankee Springs can be reached from Hastings by heading west on M-37, then turning onto Gun Lake Road for 10 miles. It can also be reached from US-131 by departing at exit 61 and following county road A-42 east for 7 miles to its junction with Gun Lake Road. The park has several campgrounds, including a modern facility on Gun Lake. Because the 212-site campground is filled throughout much of the summer, it's considerably easier to obtain a site in the park's Deep Lake Campground, a rustic facility of 120 sites.

Hall Lake Trail is the loop to Graves Hill and its trailhead is marked across from the entrance of Long Lake Outdoor Center. By heading up the right-hand fork of the immediate junction, you pass through pines and arrive at the shores of Hall Lake in 0.3 mile. Blue triangles mark the path, which crosses a bridge to skirt the lake for the next 0.25 mile, providing good views of the islands in the middle and any anglers who might be fishing for bass or bluegill.

At the northwest corner of the lake, the trail begins to climb gradually and then leaves the water view for a sharper ascent to the high point. The steepest section is just before you reach the top, but even that can be handled by most five- and six-year-old children. It's a mile to the top of Graves Hill, marked by several large rocks, the largest of which is strategically placed so young hikers can obtain a better view. From the overlook you can see the wooded interior of the state recreation area and a portion of Gun Lake.

You can extend the hike another mile by descending to the parking area nearby and following the park road. At the junction follow the right-hand fork along a road so sandy it's amazing any vehicles make it up here at all. Within a half mile the road ends at a parking area on the edge of Devils Soup Bowl, a deep and very steep, wooded depression, also the result of glacial activity.

The return trail begins as a log staircase that descends sharply from the top of Graves Hill. Once you reach the bottom, a well-beaten path heads straight for the park road. But the trail swings southwest (left) into the woods. You hug the road briefly, even hike a ridge above it at one point, then swing away to pass a small meadow. Blue markers lead you through an impressive oak forest and past views of a larger meadow. The trail descends between it and a third open area, reenters pine forest, and climbs a hill a quarter mile from the trailhead. You're skirting the road at this point, but unless a car goes by, you'd never know it. After passing a major junction for cross-country skiers, you emerge at the trailhead.

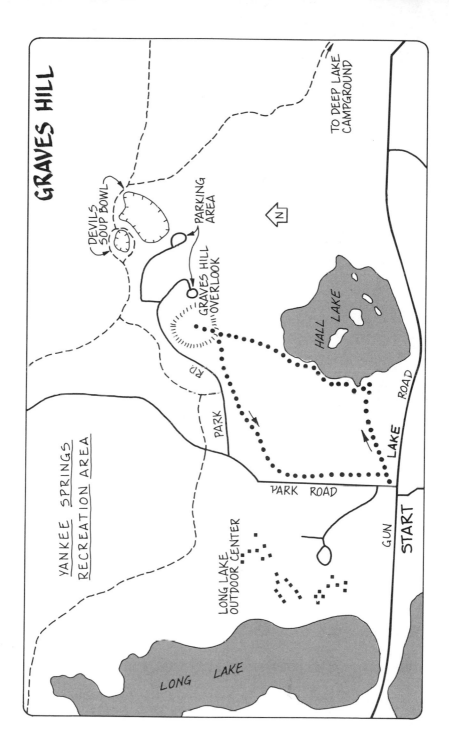

GRAVES HILL

TO DEEP LAKE CAMPGROUND

DEVILS SOUP BOWL

PARKING AREA

N

GRAVES HILL OVERLOOK

HALL LAKE

PARK RD

LAKE ROAD

PARK ROAD

YANKEE SPRINGS RECREATION AREA

LONG LAKE OUTDOOR CENTER

GUN

START

LONG LAKE

Cyclists cross a trail bridge on the bicycle path, Hudson Mills Metropark

13. HUDSON MILLS

HUDSON MILLS METROPARK

Activity: Bicycling
County: Washtenaw
Difficulty: Easy
Length: 3-mile loop
Fee: Vehicle entry fee
Information: Park headquarters, (313) 426-8211

In 1827, Cornelius Osterhout built a sawmill along the banks of the Huron River in a spot where he thought there was enough current to power the large waterwheel. There was, and by the early 1880s a gristmill, cider mill, and plaster mill were added to the hamlet of Hudson Mills. Today the mill town is gone, but what you will find in its place is Hudson Mills Metropark, the destination of an easy outdoor bicycle trip that combines a ride through the woods with scenic views of Huron River and even a side trip to poke around the ruins of the old mills.

The 1,624-acre park is 6 miles north of Ann Arbor and reached from US-23 by departing west on North Territorial Road (exit 49) and following it for 7 miles to the posted entrance. The paved bicycle trail is a 3-mile loop that can be picked up at a number of locations, but the best place might be at the park's activity center where there are modern restrooms, food service, an information office, and an indoor eating area. The center also rents out 20-inch and 26-inch single-speed bicycles, as well as 26-inch tandem bicycles, from spring through fall 10:00 A.M. until 5:00 P.M. daily.

The bike path crosses the entrance drive to the activities center and by heading north you cut through a grassy field and then emerge at Oak Meadows picnic area, where you come to a road crossing. To the north (right) is the entrance drive to Rapids View picnic area, the site of a state historic marker dedicated to the mills. From a spot 20 yards north (right) of the marker you can view the rapids (most impressive during the spring high water) and the stone foundation of Birkett Mill on the opposite bank.

For a closer view of the remains, leave the bikes behind and follow the canoe portage to North Territorial Road bridge. Cross the river and look for the unmarked dirt path leading south (left) along the other bank. All that remains of the mill is the stone foundation of its basement, but if you peer closely into the river, you will see what appears to be railroad ties that were used to direct the current into the waterwheel. The large wheel was positioned on the largest island, and with a little imagination and some coaxing, most children can visualize the operation by which three men produced 6,000 barrels of flour a year from the gristmill alone.

The bike path, meanwhile, heads west past the tables and shelter of the River Grove picnic area, and then swings south to cross a wooden bridge onto a large island that splits the Huron River into two channels. It's a quick pedal to a second bridge off the island and at this point you enter the wooded section of the trail—a scenic ride of more than a mile through hardwood forest, with an occasional bench and view of the river. You may even see someone fishing along the banks for bass, perch, or panfish.

After 2 miles you reach a scenic and little-used picnic area along a river bend, at which point the path enters a grassy field to swing past the parking area of Pine View picnic area. The activities center, visible from here, is only a short ride away.

14. THE LEDGES
FITZGERALD COUNTY PARK

Activity: Day hike
County: Eaton
Difficulty: Easy
Length: 1 mile one way
Fee: Vehicle entry fee
Information: Park office, (517) 627-7351

■ Grand Ledge, the only place to do any serious climbing in Michigan, also makes for a fun adventure for children, even if they're years away from lacing up a pair of rock shoes. The town west of Lansing is named after "The Ledges," towering faces of sheer rock that border the Grand River. These ancient sedimentary outcroppings have become a popular re-creational and educational area because of their unique geological formation.

Rock climbers gather at Oak Park at the end of West Front Street on the north side of the river; you can watch as they pursue their sport there through much of the summer. Families should head to the south side for a far less danger-ous adventure—a mile hike along the river that provides a close-up view of The Ledges. One end of the trail is Island Park, located in the heart of downtown Grand Ledge.

But the best place to start and end is Fitzgerald Park, an Eaton County park located 1.5 miles west of town at 3808 Grand Ledge Highway. The 78-acre unit borders the Grand

River and features six picnic sites, nature trails, a fish ladder, and a small nature center that is open May through October 1:00 to 5:00 P.M. on Wednesday, Saturday, and Sunday. On the other side of the park, just east of the barn theater, is the start of the Ledges Trail, marked by a box with interpretive brochures.

The first portion of the trail lies in the park and has eleven numbered posts. You quickly descend a stairway and cross a bridge over Sandstone Creek to reach the first set of ledges on the other side. The impressive rock cliffs were formed 270 million years ago when most of Michigan was covered by water that carried and deposited sediments (sand, silt, and clay) in layers along river banks and beaches. After time and pressure compacted the layers into rock, the Grand River sculptured the cliffs through years of erosion.

Post number 11 is at the railroad trestle that marks the

The ledges along the Grand River, Fitzgerald County Park

boundary of Fitzgerald Park. From here the trail crosses private property and one house does come into view. But most of the time the level trail is a secluded walk among hemlock pines with the Grand River lapping on one side and the stone cliffs on the other. At 0.5 mile, or the halfway point of the path, you can view the steepest ledges towering 70 feet above the north bank of the river. Bring a pair of binoculars and you can sit and watch climbers slowly inch their way up the face.

The trail ends at Island Park, where an old iron bridge crosses the river to the second island of what used to be the Seven Islands Resorts, a popular vacation spot at the turn of the century. Today the long island in the Grand River has benches, picnic tables, and small docks along it, as well as a flock of resident ducks eager for a handout of bread.

15.
HOISTER
LAKE
AU SABLE STATE FOREST

Activities: Day hike, camping
County: Gladwin
Difficulty: Easy
Length: Loops of 1.7 and 2.7 miles
Fee: Camping fee
Information: DNR Gladwin office, (517) 426-9205

■ Heading up north and need a place to camp the first night? A short side trip from US-27 or I-75 is Trout Lake within the Au Sable State Forest south of Houghton Lake. The lightly used recreation area includes a picnic area, pathway, undeveloped boat launch, and several campgrounds where you can usually get a shoreline site, even on the weekends. A night spent here can be an adventure (just getting here is an adventure), with an opportunity to hike around

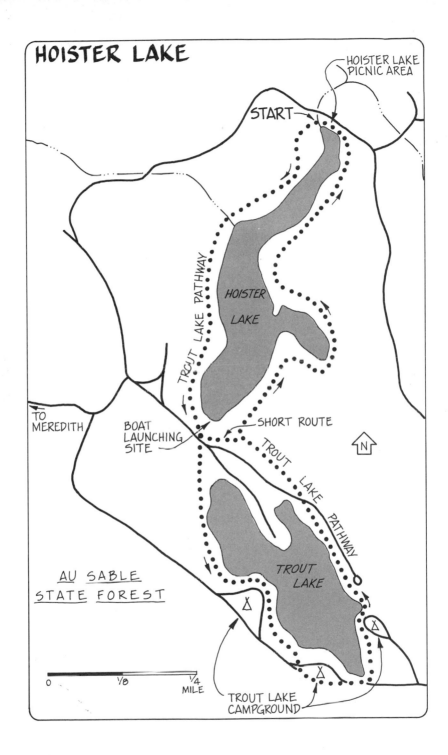

HOISTER LAKE

HOISTER LAKE
PICNIC AREA

START

TROUT LAKE PATHWAY

HOISTER
LAKE

TO
MEREDITH

BOAT
LAUNCHING
SITE

SHORT ROUTE

TROUT LAKE PATHWAY

N

TROUT
LAKE

AU SABLE
STATE FOREST

0   ⅛   ¼
MILE

TROUT LAKE
CAMPGROUND

Hoister Lake, fish Trout Lake, or spot a variety of wildlife, including porcupines, deer, or possibly a bald eagle.

The easiest way to reach the area is to exit onto M-61 either from I-75 (exit 190) or from US-27 at Harrison. Follow the state highway into Gladwin where you turn north onto M-18 to reach Meredith. It's 15 miles to the small town, but a scenic drive as the road winds through a rolling countryside of patchwork farms and stands of hardwoods. In Meredith, turn east onto Meredith Grade Road for 1.5 miles, then north on a dirt road that is posted "State Forest Campground." Follow this road 0.8 mile, but be careful: it's badly rutted and frequently washes out after a hard rain. You'll arrive at a junction in the middle of the woods with a sign telling you that Hoister Lake Picnic Area is a mile north and Trout Lake Campground is to the south.

The campground is nice, with a number of sites overlooking the water at the lake's south end. You can also pick up the Trout Lake Pathway here and follow it 2.7 miles around both Trout and Hoister lakes. But the best portion is the 1.7-mile loop around Hoister, which can be picked up from the picnic area at the north end of that lake. Most of this loop follows the ridges that enclose Hoister, providing good views for almost the entire walk.

The picnic area includes parking, vault toilets, and a small dock on the lake, while nearby a blue arrow on a huge red pine points the way to the trail along the lake's west shoreline. The walk begins with an immediate ascent of a log stairway which tops out on a ridge bordering Hoister's narrow northern half. The trail follows the ridge, providing a superb view of the water below before descending and crossing a large stream. For the next quarter mile you pass through a cedar swamp and cross two more small streams where things can get wet at times. You return to skirting the edge of the lake at its south end before emerging at an undeveloped boat launch 0.8 mile from the picnic area.

The blue blazes and off-road-vehicle (ORV) trails can make it a little confusing here, as one trail veers off to cross the entrance road on its way to the Trout Lake Campground. If you are returning to the picnic area, just stay close to the water and you will reach the launch easily to see the trail resume on the other side. The trail begins with a steep climb up a ridge before skirting the lake's southeast corner for another good view of the water from above. This is pleasant hiking and stays this way for 0.4 mile, at which point the trail descends to skirt around a marshy bay off the lake.

Spend some time along the shores of the bay, if the mosquitoes don't drive you away, to see a variety of wildlife, including waterfowl, turtles sunning themselves on logs, and even bass on a still night rising to the surface to engulf a bug. From the bay the trail climbs steeply to the ridge again, allowing you to view the narrow portion of the lake and the hilly terrain off to the north. In a little more than 0.5 mile, the trail drops off the ridge to the ORV barriers that encircle the picnic area.

16.
RENT-A-TIPI

WILSON STATE PARK

Activity: Camping
County: Clare
Difficulty: Easy
Fee: Vehicle entry permit, tent rental fee
Information: Park headquarters, (517) 539-3021

■ The little boy didn't have a six-shooter, but he did arrive at Wilson State Park with a ten-gallon hat. Also a plastic tomahawk. And, of course, he was wearing his cowboy boots. All were necessary items for his family's weekend stay in the park's Rent-A-Tipi. His folks brought along the sleeping bags, food, pots, toothbrushes. . . .

Rent-A-Tipi is the newest angle to the state parks' Rent-A-Tent program and there might not be a better way to lure children out of their bedrooms and into a tent for a night or two. Park officials call the structures "authentic tribal replicas," though it's doubtful many Indians had canvas cots to sleep on back in the 1800s. The base of the tent is a wooden platform, 20 feet in diameter, encircled by fifteen 24-foot poles lashed together to support the canvas.

At Wilson State Park, the tipi has five cots inside and a picnic table and fire pit outside. For a small additional fee you can also rent a Coleman propane stove, cooler, and an electric lantern. You need to bring bedding, cookware, tableware, water jug, rain gear, flashlights, and food.

Rent-a-Tent was established to encourage people with little or no camping experience to spend a night in the woods without having to first invest in a lot of equipment. Rent-A-Tipi, however, has attracted families more than inexperienced campers. Children love the adventure, as it ignites in their imaginations images of the Old West and other childhood fantasies. "We even have grandparents renting the tipi to enjoy it with their grandchildren," said one park ranger.

Campers at a Rent-A-Tipi in the Michigan State Park system

Because of the program's popularity, you should reserve the tipi well in advance, especially in July when it's booked almost every day. The tipi is set up from May 1 to October 1, and there is a two-night minimum stay. You can reserve it by calling the park or obtaining a "Michigan State Park Tent/Tipi Application" and mailing it in with the current fee. Many families who want to secure July dates make their reservations in March or April.

The Wilson State Park is located 1 mile north of Harrison right off Business US-27. The 38-acre park overlooks Burt Lake and features modern toilets with showers, a picnic area with play equipment, and a beach and designated swimming area that is sandy and shallow. Other state parks that offer Rent-A-Tipis are Holly Recreation Area (313-634-8811), Pontiac Lake Recreation Area (313-666-1020), Interlochen State Park (616-276-9511), and Burt Lake (616-238-9392) in the Lower Peninsula. In the Upper Peninsula, Indian Lake State Park (906-341-2355), Baraga State Park (906-353-6558), and Bewabic State Park (906-875-3324) also have them.

17.
SILVER CREEK
PATHWAY
PERE MARQUETTE STATE FOREST

Activities: Day hike, camping
County: Lake
Difficulty: Easy to moderate
Length: Loops of 1.5 and 2.5 miles
Fee: Camping fee
Information: DNR field office in Baldwin, (616) 745-4651

■ Summer is . . . a rope swing. A thick line tied to a maple tree leaning over the Pine River. Its frazzled end touches the surface of a deep pool, while farther up are several strategically placed double-knots for small hands to grasp during the pendulum swing out to middle of the river.

For years, families have come to the Silver Creek State Forest Campground in the Pere Marquette State Forest to escape the heat and bustle of the city down south. They set up a tent or the trailer in one of the shaded campsites lining the banks of the Pine River so parents or grandparents can sit in folding chairs and toss baited hooks into the waters famous for rainbow and brown trout. The children wander to their rope swing at the beginning of the Silver Creek Pathway, for a refreshing dip and a little horseplay in a natural swimming hole located where Silver Creek spills into the Pine River.

The campground is rustic (vault toilets, no electricity) but scenic and usually not too busy. Almost half of the twenty-nine sites are either along the Pine River or three steps away. The facility is located north of Baldwin and west of Cadillac and from US-131 is reached by exiting onto Luther Highway and heading west for Luther, the small town on the banks of the Little Manistee River. At Luther head north on State Road for 5.5 miles and look for the posted entrance of the campground.

The trailhead for the pathway is located next to campsite number 10 and is posted with a display map. The trail can be either an easy 1.5-mile hike or, if continued along the east side of State Road, a 2.5-mile loop of moderate difficulty. The most scenic section by far is the first mile on the west side of the road.

Immediately after the trailhead, you come to the rope swing and a bridge over Silver Creek near its mouth. If the rest of your party can resist the temptation to end the hike there, cross the bridge where four trails lead off in four different directions. Luckily, one is marked with a blue pathway triangle and leads you across a bridge over a much smaller stream and then up a steep climb to the edge of the bluffs that line Pine River.

For the next 0.3 mile the trail follows the edge of the bluff, breaking out every now and then to good overviews of the river flowing 70 feet below you, at the base of the steep side of the bluff. Deer frequent the area, so when you're not looking at the water, keep an eye on the forest to the east. At 0.5 mile, a trail veers off to the northwest (left) and makes a

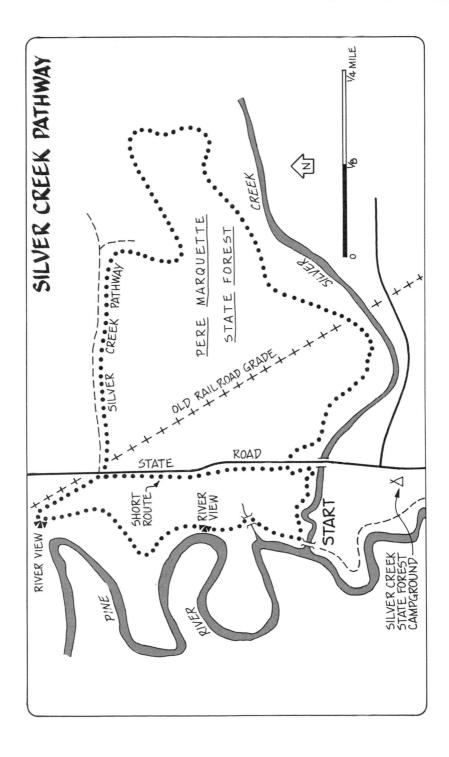

SILVER CREEK PATHWAY

sharp descent. This path was formed by anglers no doubt and should be followed only if you want to reach the river. The pathway at this point veers northeast (right) and is marked not only with blue DNR triangles but also with red ribbons, as it was recut in 1989. It stays on the bluff, coming shortly to the best view, overlooking two bends in the river and a ridge several miles away.

From here the pathway emerges at an old railroad grade that now looks like a smooth four-wheel-drive track. A post with a blue dot directs you to swing southeast (right) and in 0.2 mile you come to State Road. Continue the short loop by walking down the paved road for 0.3 mile. The long loop is marked across the road by a blue dot post and starts off by following a motor-sport trail before curving off into the woods. The trail is well marked but not used nearly as much as the shorter loop, and at times you have to search for the next post. Much of the second half, however, follows Silver Creek and makes for a scenic walk.

Both loops merge right before State Road crosses Silver Creek. On the west side of the road, at the end of a guard rail, a sign post points out where the trail enters the woods. You begin with a short descent and then follow the trail as it parallels the road briefly to the edge of the creek where there are a series of rapids and a small waterfall. The trail swings west here and in a couple hundred yards arrives at the bridge and rope swing near the mouth of Silver Creek. Time for a swim.

18. MARL LAKE
SOUTH HIGGINS STATE PARK

Activities: Day hike, skiing
County: Roscommon
Difficulty: Easy
Length: Loops of 2.0, 3.5, and 5.5 miles
Fee: Vehicle entry permit
Information: Park headquarters, (517) 821-6374

■ Situated on the east side of County Road 100 is an escape from the campers, crowds, and, during the winter, snowmobiles that are the trademark of South Higgins Lake State Park. Marl Lake is the other half of the state park and offers a quiet wooded path that wraps around the shoreline for a scenic but easy day hike in the summer or a level ski when the ground is blanketed in snow. In autumn the hardwood trees that are scattered throughout the white and red pine provide brilliant fall colors, and early in the morning you might spot deer anywhere along the route.

The trail is divided into three loops of various lengths, with the shortest an ideal first day hike, even for children as young as four or five. Only 2 miles long and extremely level, the loop hugs Marl Lake so closely for the first half that there is a water view from every step. The second loop is 3.5 miles and reaches a bench on the lakeshore—a scenic spot for lunch—before heading back. The complete loop, a 5.5-mile round-trip to the Cut River, passes through swamp area that isn't planked and can be rather muddy in the spring.

To reach the trail from I-75, exit at Roscommon (exit 239) but head south away from the town and immediately turn west (right) onto County Road 103 where there is a state park sign. Follow CO-103 for 3 miles and then turn south (left) onto CO-100 for 3 more miles. The Marl Lake parking lot is located right before the main entrance to the state park on the east side of CO-100.

At the parking area are picnic tables and a large trail sign, as well as a view of the lake. The trail can be walked easily in tennis shoes, but it's best to leave any fishing equipment in the car. There's perch, northern pike, and bass in these waters, but the lake is shallow, no more than 3 feet deep anywhere, and successful anglers usually are those who boat out to the middle. The trail begins at a bridge and from there heads south as a wooded path, hugging the lake for the first 0.75 mile and providing delightful views of the water through the fringe of pine trees.

Right before the first cutoff, you cross two long bridges that provide dry access between the lake to the east and an interesting swamp to the west. The cutoff is posted with green dots swinging south to the return loop and red dots continuing along the lakeshore. The 3.5-mile red loop veers slightly away from the lake, offering only occasional glimpses of the water until you reach the second cutoff in a little over a 0.5 mile. At this junction, a path descends to a bench along the shore and from there you can look directly across the lake and see where you began the adventure.

Did we really hike all that way?

The red dots head east (right) to the return portion of the loop and the blue dots continue north, swinging even farther away from the lake. Occasionally a blue triangle marks the trail, which arrives at a bench about 0.75 mile from the red cutoff. From there it's an easy walk down to the banks of the Cut River, which flows between Higgins Lake and Houghton Lake to the south.

The return trip on the loop follows an old vehicle track and is considerably wider than the first half. It winds through hardwoods, completely out of view of the lake and is longer— a 3.3-mile walk back to the parking area—and not nearly as interesting. Some families, not bothered by backtracking, choose to return along the shorter shoreline portion, a hike of only 2.3 miles, to enjoy the views of the lake once more.

WINTER USE

From late December through February the entire route is groomed once a week for skiers and becomes an ideal run for children. There's an occasional low rise but no hilly portions to fret over. If you need to rent ski equipment, then head north (right) onto CO-100; just up the road is Cross Country Ski Headquarters (517-821-5868). The nordic ski center is open daily November through mid-March. Its hours are 9:00 A.M. to 6:00 P.M. Tuesday through Thursday and Sunday, and until 9:00 P.M. Friday, Saturday, and Monday.

Opposite: *Swing bridge over the South Fork Cass River, Sanilac State Historic Site*

LAKE
HURON

19.
SANILAC
PETROGLYPHS
SANILAC STATE HISTORIC SITE

Activity: Day hike
County: Sanilac
Difficulty: Easy
Length: 1.5-mile loop
Fee: None
Information: Port Crescent State Park, (517) 738-8663

■ Woods, a gentle stream, the possibility of encountering wildlife, and easy hiking are why the trail in Sanilac State Historic Site is such a good family outing. But what makes it an excellent adventure for children is the way the historic artifacts fill young minds with images of ancient hunters, Indian villages, and nineteenth-century loggers.

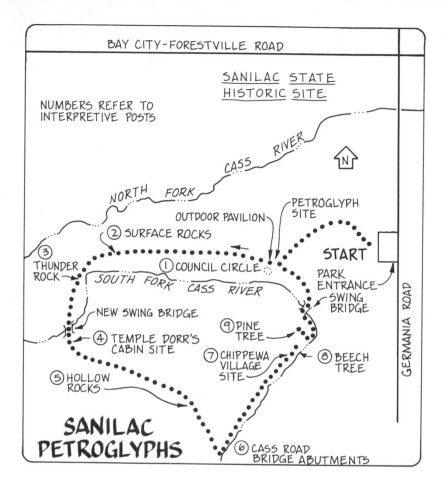

SANILAC PETROGLYPHS

The park is located 13 miles south of Bad Axe. From M-53 head east onto Bay City-Forestville Road to a posted corner on Germania Road. The entrance is a half mile south on Germania, but you'll need to pick up the key from a nearby farmhouse. Directions to the farmhouse are posted at the park entrance.

The key provides entry into an outdoor pavilion that covers the main feature of the park—petroglyphs. These 1,000-year-old aboriginal rock carvings, the only ones ever found in Michigan, were cut into a large slab of sandstone. Even children can guess the most prominent one—a bowman with a long, single arm depicting both his arm and arrow—

and it's fun trying to figure out what the rest could be. Deer? Hunters? Mythological creatures, maybe?

With such a great start to the walk, some young hikers head up the trail half expecting a tipi around every bend. Eight interpretive posts line the route. The first, a few steps from the rock carvings, shows where the "council circle" was located for a Chippewa tribe that once had a village in the park. In 0.25 mile, the second post points out some surface rocks with large round depressions believed to be mortars that Indians made to store and protect food. The mortars were easy to make—the Indians simply pounded the soft sandstone with round, hard rocks. Larger mortars are at Thunder Rock, the third stop.

At this point the trail curves south, close to South Fork Cass River, and passes through a lowland forest. The large maple trees arching over the river are impressive in the fall, but come spring this can be a muddy section. The moisture and mud, however, encourage a profusion of wildflowers in May and June, when the trails are criss-crossed with easy-to-identify deer tracks leading off in every direction.

In a little more than a half mile from the pavilion, the trail crosses a swing bridge over the river; on the other side interpretive post number 4 marks an earthen mound that was the foundation of Temple Dorr's cabin, a timber cruiser who lived here in 1835. Just up the trail is a rock cropping down which loggers once rolled logs into the river, to float them to the Saginaw mills. The trail passes some impressive birch trees and then emerges into a semiopen area for the remainder of the hike. It was here (post number 7) that the Chippewa village was located. As late as 1900 Indians from a Caro reservation spent the summer months here while they picked and dried wild berries. If you search around, you can find more mortars.

The impressive pine nearby is a lone survivor of the Great Fire of 1881, an event that closed the chapter on logging in Michigan's Thumb region. From the towering pine (great place for a snack), you return to the river at a well-built beaver dam and then, just below the structure, cross to the other bank on another swing bridge. The pavilion is now only minutes away.

20.
HURON
SAND DUNES
PORT CRESCENT STATE PARK

Activities: Day hike, camping
County: Huron
Difficulty: Medium
Length: 2.3-mile loop
Fee: Vehicle entry fee, camping fee
Information: Port Crescent State Park, (517) 738-8663

■ The sand dunes along Lake Huron can't compare in stature with those along the west side of Michigan. But to hikers with short legs and small arms, the dunes in Port Crescent State Park are soft mountains to be climbed and conquered. Parents are usually equally impressed with the sweeping panoramas that the high perches of sand provide. This excellent hike combines the dunes and good views with a woodland walk; as part of an overnight stay in the park's beachside campground, it makes for a wonderful outdoor weekend for families.

Keep in mind, however, that the Port Crescent State Park is an extremely popular campground from late June through August, so it's best either to arrive Monday through Wednesday or book a site in advance by calling the park office. The park is located 5 miles west of Port Austin on M-25 and is split in half by the Pinnebog River, with the trail in the eastern half. One trailhead is the old iron bridge at the corner of M-25 and Port Crescent Road, providing direct access to both the blue loop (1.3 miles) and the red loop (1.1 miles).

But most children prefer starting at the other trailhead, located in the campground across from the modern restroom and between two beachfront sites. At this beautiful beach on Saginaw Bay, you'll want to kick off your shoes or boots and scramble around the mouth of the Old Pinnebog River Channel. Then head toward the yellow posts and there they are . . . the first of many small dunes of sand. If the sun is out and the temperatures warm, it's hard for children to resist the temptation of rolling down the sandy mounds.

The short yellow spur ascends to the first scenic vista and bench, offering views of the old river channel and the campground below. From there the blue loop begins. You can descend south along the old channel or, to hike the most impressive section of the trail first, go west through a wooded ravine.

Heading west, you remain away from the water and sand for 0.3 mile. Keep an eye out for blue diamonds on the trees as the trail turns sharply north to return within view of the bay and more of the open dunes that border it. In another

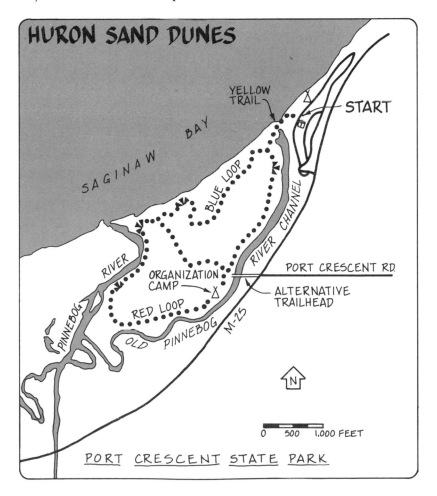

0.25 mile you'll reach the junction of the red and blue loops, marked by a large pole and another bench. Follow the blue markers south and then north along the river channel to return to the yellow spur and reduce the walk to 1.8 miles.

But continue west for more views. Follow the red poles and diamonds and soon you'll emerge at another bench with a panorama of the mouth of the Pinnebog River, the shoreline along the Saginaw Bay, and the park's stretch of open dunes. It's the best view in the park, but the steep drop of sand at your feet is what will intrigue young hikers. Wouldn't it be fun just to run down and . . .

For the next 0.4 mile the trail continues along this sandy bluff with the river below, until it reaches one final bench where you can see much of the Pinnebog and the wetlands it flows through. At this point the trail swings to a southerly direction and then to the east, becoming a walk through woods. In another 0.4 mile you reach the organization camp (vault toilets and a picnic shelter) and then the junction at the old iron bridge. Drop down toward the bridge to pick up the blue loop, which follows the old channel before climbing up to the junction with the yellow spur.

21.
PERCH
CHARTERS
SAGINAW BAY

Activity: Fishing
County: Huron
Difficulty: Moderate
Fee: Per person charter fee
Information: Thumb Marine Charters, (517) 738-5271 or Caseville Resort, (517) 856-2323

■ They're called party boats, but these perch charters on Saginaw Bay can be pretty serious stuff, especially for a budding young angler. The boats are so named because they take

Happy anglers on board a perch party boat in Saginaw Bay

anywhere from twenty to thirty anglers from one reef in the bay to the next until they find a "mess of yellow bellies" on the bottom. Then the fishing can be fast and furious, leading to an evening feast of the most delectable fillets the Great Lakes offers.

Perch fishing is legendary on Saginaw Bay and party boats run daily from Memorial Day to Labor Day out of the harbors of Caseville and Port Austin, 19 miles apart on M-25 near the tip of Michigan's Thumb. It's first-come-first-on-board for either the 7:30 A.M. morning run or the afternoon trip that departs between 1:30 and 2:30 P.M. The adventure lasts 4 hours, more than enough time to fill a bucket if the fish are feeding.

Perch fishing is the next logical step for six- or seven-year-old anglers who already have tried their hands at catching panfish from a stationary boat or dock. The party boats are large enough for children to get up and walk around if they want. Captains and first mates help anglers bait minnows, land fish, or untangle lines (a common mishap on a crowded party boat). And best of all, there's a bathroom on board.

Compared to lake trout or salmon charters, it's an affordable adventure, even if the whole family decides to go. Most boats have reduced rates for weekdays, senior citizen rates, and special prices for families.

Perch fishing is not difficult to master but, unlike fishing on salmon charters, it does involve working a rod and being attuned to hungry fish trying to swipe your minnow. Bait is included in the charter fee and you can rent a pole, but it's best to bring along your own, with a few "perch rigs" with No. 4 or No. 6 hooks.

A perch rig is a swivel, monofilament line, from which two short leaders extend with the hooks. You clip a weight onto the bottom. The idea is to hook two minnows so the barbs don't show, and then toss the rig overboard when the boat stops at a reef. Let the weight hit the bottom anywhere from 10 to 40 feet down, raise it an inch or two, and then be ready!

If the perch are hungry, there is no problem feeling that distinct series of tugs that means a fish is swiping the minnow. But many times the hit is extremely light, and only those with sensitive fingers—who feel the hit and immediately set the hook—will end up catching fish. At times like this, anglers must constantly check their hooks to make sure they still have bait.

Even if you don't catch a bucket of perch, the cruise on a nice day is enjoyable and the scenery excellent. The boat is almost always within sight of the shore, providing views of the sand dunes at Port Crescent State Park (see 20. Huron Sand Dunes) from an unusual vantage point. Besides, if you don't catch a bucketful, then you won't have to clean them . . . and you'll be thankful for that.

22.
SHIAWASSEE
WATERFOWL TRAIL
SHIAWASSEE NATIONAL WILDLIFE REFUGE

Activities: Day hike, birding
County: Saginaw
Difficulty: Moderate
Length: 5-mile loop
Fee: None
Information: Refuge headquarters, (517) 777-5930

■ The Waterfowl Trail in the Shiawassee National Wildlife Refuge is an interesting walk almost any time of the year, as it provides dry footing through an area of marshes, ponds, and other moist soil units managed for a variety of wildlife. But during the peak migration seasons of March through April and September through early November, this day hike offers an impressive view of waterfowl, especially Canada geese.

At the height of migration, some 25,000 to 40,000 geese and 50,000 ducks gather on the refuge. From the observation tower, the halfway point of the 5-mile hike, you can watch flocks of hundreds rise in unison off the water, circle the refuge twice, and then depart. You are also sure to spot muskrats and possibly a variety of other wildlife, including great blue heron, great egrets, or some 200 other species of birds, as well as beaver or even white-tailed deer.

The refuge is south of Saginaw and reached from I-75 by exiting west on M-46 (exit 149) and then south on M-13 for 6 miles to Curtis Road. Turn west onto Curtis Road and in 0.75 mile reach the refuge headquarters at the corner of Mower Road. The headquarters is open Monday through Friday 8:00 A.M. to 5:00 P.M., but an outside information box with trail brochures is provided for weekend hikers and others. The trailhead is another 3.5 miles west at the end of Curtis Road where you turn north to reach a parking area and trail sign.

Calling it a trail is a little misleading. What you are walk-

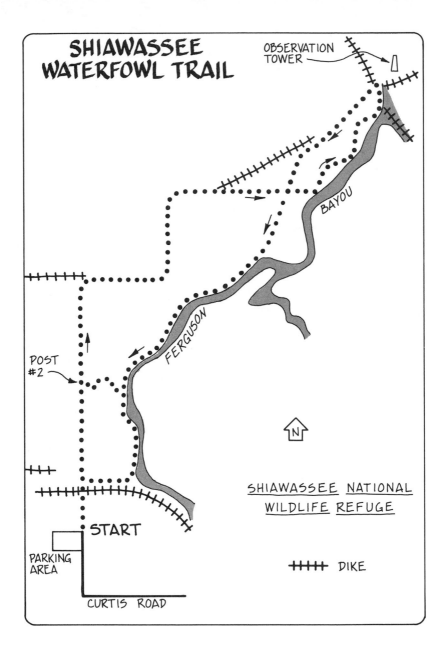

SHIAWASSEE WATERFOWL TRAIL

OBSERVATION TOWER

BAYOU

FERGUSON

POST #2

START

PARKING AREA

CURTIS ROAD

N

SHIAWASSEE NATIONAL WILDLIFE REFUGE

++++ DIKE

ing on most of the time is a series of dikes that form a maze through this 9,800-acre refuge. On either side of you might be a marsh, a flooded pond, a wooded area, or a field of corn planted to provide food for waterfowl. Most likely you'll see dozens of muskrats swimming in ponds or scurrying down the dikes, but keep a sharp eye out for ducks, other birds, turtles, or the downed trees that were gnawed by beavers.

The trail features twelve interpretive posts, which correspond to explanations in the brochure. Within 0.5 mile of the start, just past post number 2, is the cutoff that shortens the walk to 1.5 miles. In another 0.5 mile, the trail begins zigzagging its way east until it crosses the return trail and then reaches Ferguson Bayou at post number 6. (Some hikers mistakenly head up the return trail before reaching the waterway.)

The observation tower is 0.5 mile away, the halfway point and a great place for lunch. The wooden structure provides an overview of the fields and ponds bordering the Shiawassee River, with more crops to the west, impounded water to the northeast, and, most likely, geese everywhere. By the hundreds or even thousands they will be waddling through vegetation, floating on the surface of ponds, or running across the water in a herculean effort to get their eight-pound bodies airborne. At peak migration, when more than 25,000 geese congregate here, the area is, as one refuge biologist said, "like O'Hare Airport at Christmas—geese are flying everywhere."

You follow a different route back from the observation tower and in 0.5 mile come to the posted junction passed earlier in the hike. From there you're still 1.75 miles from the trailhead, with much of the walk bordering the green tree reservoir, a forest flooded each spring by meltwater runoff.

23.
HIGHBANKS
TRAIL
HURON NATIONAL FOREST

Activities: Day hike, skiing
County: Iosco
Difficulty: Moderate to challenging
Length: 7 miles one way
Fee: None
Information: Tawas Ranger District, (517) 362-4477

■ Strung along the towering bluffs above the Au Sable River is the Highbanks Trail, a skiing and hiking route that was developed through the Corsair Ski Council and the Huron National Forest. This is a point-to-point trail and, without two vehicles, it's almost impossible to avoid backtracking. Also, the route winds close to River Road at times, and the sound of cars speeding by occasionally breaks up the peaceful tranquility of the wooded path.

But the drawbacks are hardly worth considering when compared with what the Highbanks Trail has to offer: outstanding scenery and views, the possibility of spotting bald eagles during the spring and summer, or a stop at the Lumbermen's Monument to learn about the life of a logger in the 1800s. With its mostly level contour along the tops of the bluffs, this trail makes an excellent outing for children, where monuments to the past and panoramas of the river keep their minds off tired feet.

The trail is rated moderate because of its overall length, but it can easily be shortened for young hikers not up to a 7-mile day. The western trailhead is located at the pull-off for Iargo Springs, a mile east of M-65 along River Road. The eastern trailhead is on a hill above Sid Town, a cluster of cabins and a store off Cooke Road a quarter mile north of River Road. In between are two more places to pick up the path—the Canoe Race Monument and, farther east, the Lumbermen's Monument. The best and easiest portion for young children is the 3.6-mile segment from Iargo Springs to Lumbermen's Monument. The hike can be further shortened to an even 1.8-mile walk by beginning at Canoe Race Monument.

You'll see the first of many spectacular views of the Au Sable River the minute you step out of your car at Iargo Springs, a historic resting place for Chippewa Indians following the Saginaw-Mackinac Trail. Along with a place to park the car, there are vault toilets, picnic shelters, and water available. If you have time, hike down to the springs, descending a staircase of almost 300 steps, with eight benches for resting. The area below is pleasant and tranquil, with the springs gurgling out of the moss-laden bluffs and into the river under a canopy of pine trees. Back at the parking area blue diamonds near the picnic shelters mark the beginning of the trail.

The path follows the edge of the Highbanks for a short spell, skirts a gully, and ends up running along the power lines. You follow this man-made intrusion until you come to another panorama of the river, at which point blue diamonds mark where the trail and electrical lines part company. The trail continues to hug the forested edge of the banks until it breaks out at Canoe Race Monument, 1.8 miles from the start. The stone monument, topped by a pair of paddles, was originally built as a memorial to Jerry Curley, who died training for the Au Sable River Canoe Marathon. Today it stands in honor of all racers who attempt the annual 150-mile event from Grayling to Oscoda, often cited as the toughest canoe race in the country.

Eagles frequent the area along the Highbanks Trail, but one of the best places to catch a glimpse of the endangered bird is at Canoe Race Monument, where an active nest is nearby. Hikers will start spotting the birds in April, and in May it's not uncommon to see adult eagles carrying to the nest steelhead trout caught from the spawning run up the Au Sable.

Departing the monument, the trail stays near the edge of the banks to round what locals call "Bird Nest Point" before returning to the power-line path in a mile and crossing two small hills. Keep an eye out for the blue diamonds, but it's hard to get lost here, even when the trail takes a hard left to swing away from the lines and enter the woods. Through the forest of stately pines, you enter a pedestrian gate and 1.8 miles from Canoe Race Monument come to the entrance drive to Lumbermen's Monument.

The famous statue of the three loggers stands at the end of the drive. Near it an interesting interpretive center features displays and hands-on exhibits devoted to the era from 1850 to 1910 when Michigan was the country's greatest wood-producing state. There is another spectacular view of the flooded Au Sable and a staircase (260 steps) to riverbanks below. The interpretive center is open 10:00 A.M. to 6:00 P.M. Saturday and Sunday from late April to mid-May, daily from mid-May to September, and then Thursday to Sunday through October.

Blue diamonds mark where the trail continues on the other side of the entrance drive. The path through the pine forest skirts around the national forest campground and the parking area for the interpretive center, then leaves the monument area through another pedestrian gate. It returns to the power-line path and at 0.3 mile from the monument area arrives at a long sand dune that slopes down to the banks of the Au Sable. This is a popular area in the summer, with hikers descending for a swim in the river or simply taking a break to bask in the sun on the sandy slope. In the final 2 miles, you encounter a few more hills before the eastern trailhead is reached on a hill overlooking the store in Sid Town.

WINTER USE

From January to mid-March the Highbanks Trail becomes an 11.4-kilometer (7.1-mile) ski run, with the stretch from Iargo Springs parking area to Lumbermen's Monument rated for novice skiers. The rest of the trail, from the monument to Sid Town, is rated for intermediate skiers, as the terrain includes more hills. The Corsair Ski Council sets the track throughout the winter, but there are no warming centers along the trail since the interpretive center at the Lumbermen's Monument is closed. Ski equipment can be rented at Nordic Sports Ski Shop (517-362-2001) at 218 West Bay in East Tawas. For a 24-hour recorded snow report, call 1-800-55-TAWAS.

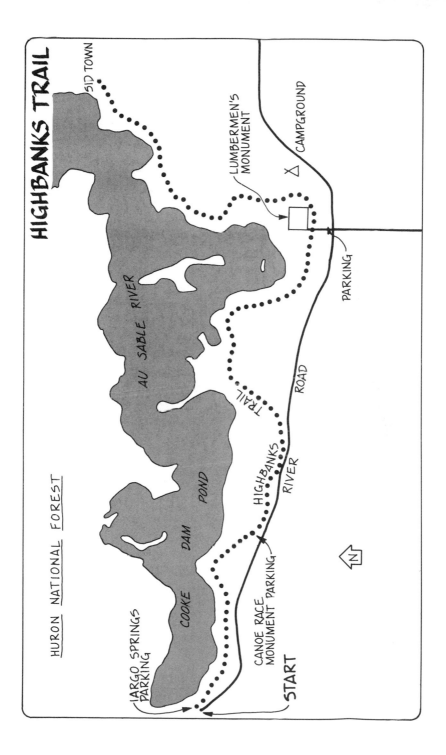

HIGHBANKS TRAIL

HURON NATIONAL FOREST

SID TOWN

AU SABLE RIVER

LUMBERMEN'S MONUMENT

CAMPGROUND

PARKING

TRAIL

HIGHBANKS

ROAD

RIVER

COOKE DAM POND

IARGO SPRINGS PARKING

CANOE RACE MONUMENT PARKING

START

N

Campers trying their luck off a fishing dock, Reid Lake, Huron National Forest

▌24. REID LAKE
HURON NATIONAL FOREST

Activities: Backpacking, fishing
County: Alcona
Difficulty: Moderate
Length: 4.2-mile loop
Fee: None
Information: Harrisville Ranger District, (517) 724-5431

■ The U.S. Forest Service manages a number of back-country areas in Michigan's four national forests to provide recreation experience free from the sights, sounds, and frantic pace of our motorized society. Among these foot-travel areas, Reid Lake in the Huron National Forest is one of the smallest, encompassing only 3,000 acres and 6 miles of gently rolling trails.

For most people, it's a day hike into the area to view or

fish the lake. But for children, the mileage is just right for an enjoyable backpacking trip, highlighted by an evening camped on the high banks above the lake or an afternoon catching small rainbow trout. Not only do the short trail distances turn Reid Lake into an excellent family backpacking trip, but the Forest Service has installed campsites, fire rings, vault toilets, and a well near the lake to make a night spent in the woods a more comfortable experience.

The foot travel area is reached from Harrisville by heading 19 miles west on M-72 to the posted entrance. From Mio, head east of M-72 21 miles to its junction with M-65 near Curran and then continue along M-72 for another 10 miles to the entrance on the south side of the state highway. At a display board at the parking area are maps and a box where you can leave your plans. Although the trail winds around several bog areas, it's surprisingly dry and can be walked in tennis shoes. Bring a lot of bug repellent in June and July, however.

There are 6.1 miles of trails around the lake. The route described here is the most scenic loop and makes for a 2.7-mile hike to a lakeside campsite the first day and then a 1.5-mile return to the parking area. To reach the junction marked by post number 2, head east (left) at the display board along a wide trail that obviously has been built to accommodate both hikers and skiers. This is a trip where you can walk two abreast most of the way.

In the first mile, the trail passes through the perfect rows of a red pine plantation, moves into a hardwood forest, and ends in a stand of paper birch. From here you make a long ascent to post number 2, 1.3 miles from the start and marked by a "You Are Here" map sign. Reid Lake is only 0.3 mile to the west (right) but head east for a much more interesting route.

Within minutes you skirt one end of Mossy Bog where it's amazing to see how much plant life one fallen log can sustain. The trail curves around the bog, ascends into a stand of paper birch, and then 1.7 miles from the trailhead passes another wet area, a green-carpeted pond with a centerpiece of standing dead trees. Sure, a few mosquitoes might be buzzing around, but even children can see there is beauty in bogs and wetlands.

The trail soon passes the rest of the bog and then ascends a low ridge to drop down to the south end of Beaver Pond, marked by an incredible dam that looks all the world like a well-laid woodpile. The trail actually crosses in front of the dam on planking and then skirts the rest of the pond itself, a body of water as big as Reid Lake. In the middle is a large lodge, while along the banks are fallen trees with the telltale signs of a beaver's handiwork—gnawed marks and wood chips around the stumps. Sit long enough on the high banks and eventually you'll see him swim by.

From the pond the trail moves into an open field, makes two sharp, well-posted ninety-degree turns, and then arrives at post number 3. To the west (left) is the Big Marsh Loop, a 1.3-mile spur around Fannies and Big marshes. Straight to the north is Reid Lake, just one low ridge away. You quickly come to post number 5 and then swing east (right) to descend to another "You Are Here" map and a "Campsites" sign. Fol-

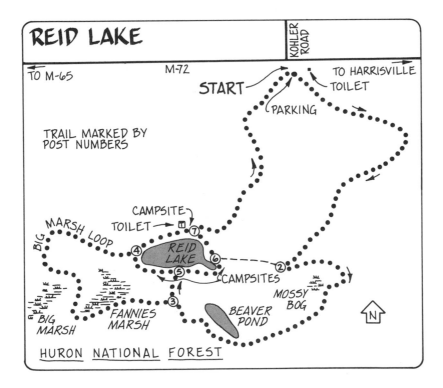

low this side trail to a pair of shaded sites situated on a bluff overlooking thc lake.

From the campsites you can see all three docks on the lake, one on the south shore and two new ones on the north shore. Reid is stocked annually with rainbow trout, but also holds good populations of panfish, especially bluegill. Trout are most often caught by anglers who take the time to haul a canoe in, but the panfish can be landed easily from the docks on the north side. For cither fish, simple rigs of small hooks, a worm, and a couple split shots are sufficient. Add a bobber if you're dock fishing for bluegill.

Back at post number 5, the trail skirts the lake around the west end and in 0.25 mile comes to post number 4, the junction with the other end of Big Marsh Loop. Head up the spur to reach the well in 100 yards or continue along the lake to pass the docks, two other campsites, and vault toilets. The Lakeshore Loop ends at post number 7, where you head inland to return to the parking area. This final leg is like a road through the woods and for the most part gently descends for almost a mile to the trailhead.

▌25.
JEWELL
LAKE
HURON NATIONAL FOREST

Activities: Day hike, camping
County: Alcona
Difficulty: Easy
Length: 1-mile loop
Fee: Camping fee
Information: Harrisville Ranger District, (517) 724-5431

█ Jewell Lake Trail may be the perfect choice for a child's first hike in the woods. Part of it winds along the shore of a crystal clear lake, part of it passes through a white forest of paper birch. There's plenty of wildlife to investigate, a

---

wooden bridge to cross, even two benches along the way to stop and rest. All this within a mile-long loop.

The trailhead is located in Huron National Forest's Jewell Lake Campground, which is reached from Harrisville by heading west on M-72 for 14.5 miles. Turn north on Sanborn Road for 1.7 miles and then left on Trask Road for 0.7 mile to the posted entrance. The facility has 32 rustic campsites, and although none are directly on the water, most of the Aspen Loop sites are only a short walk from a small, sandy beach on Jewell Lake. The campground makes this a possible weekend destination for hiking, swimming, and fishing the lake for easy-to-catch bluegill and other panfish. Dad and mom, however, can set their sights on largemouth bass or northern pike.

The trail is posted on the west side of the beach area and skirts the lake to a log bridge where children can stand in the middle and view a beaver dam below. On the other side you resume skirting the lake. Take time to stop often and study the edge of the shore. Jewell Lake is extremely clear and offers a good view of an underwater world teeming with life. Large snails scour the sandy bottom, frogs leap in at the

Beach at Jewell Lake Campground, Huron National Forest

sound of footsteps, and panfish are almost always visible darting toward the middle of the lake. Tell the children to sneak up slowly to see fish hovering within an arm's length of the shore, along a log, or under a root or other structure that gives them a sense of security.

At 0.2 mile you come to the junction with the return trail and then the first of two benches. The trail continues to hug the shoreline, providing nice views of the lake or more opportunities for shoreline investigations. At 0.5 mile you reach another bench and the trail swings into a woods of predominately paper birch and aspen. But along the ground you'll see the next generation of forest popping up through layers of decaying leaves—small pine saplings, maybe only two or three inches high. You wander through the woods for 0.3 mile before returning to the lake and backtracking to the beach and trailhead.

26.
KIRTLAND'S
WARBLER TOUR
HURON NATIONAL FOREST

Activity: Birding
County: Oscoda and Roscommon
Difficulty: Easy
Length: 1- to 2-mile tours
Fee: None
Information: Mio Ranger District (517) 826-3252, or DNR Grayling Field Office (517) 348-6371

■ The state bird may be the robin, but birders across the country know Michigan best as the home of the Kirtland's warbler. The small bird is the size of a sparrow and features a distinct yellow breast, a bobbing tail, and what one biologist described as a "liquid, bubbling song." The species was almost extinct in the late 1970s and today its entire population fluctuates around 200.

The songbird spends its winters in obscurity in the Bahamas, where it is rarely seen. But come spring the warbler migrates to Michigan, arriving in mid-May to nest almost exclusively in the jack pines of the Lower Peninsula. Remarkably, during May and June eighty percent of the world's total population of Kirtland's warblers is contained in two Michigan counties, Oscoda and Roscommon.

The nesting areas are closed to the public, but sighting the rare bird is possible through a "Kirtland's Warbler Tour." These last 1.5 to 2 hours and are sponsored by the U.S. Forest Service office in Mio and the state Department of Natural Resources office in Grayling from mid-May through July 4. The Mio office is located just north of the town on M-33 and offers the field trip Wednesday, Thursday, and Friday at 7:30 P.M., and Saturday and Sunday at 7:30 A.M. and 11:00 A.M. The Grayling DNR office is reached by following Business I-75 (exit 254 or 259) off the interstate highway into town and then turning east at Michigan Avenue past the hospital. At Grayling the tours are offered at 7:00 and 11:00 A.M. daily.

This activity is not strenuous, but young children under the age of seven tend to lose interest quickly in a bird that is neither as big nor as impressive as a Canada goose or a bald eagle. But the tour will fascinate older children intrigued by Michigan's wildlife and is famous among birders who come from around the country for their only glimpse of a Kirtland's warbler.

The tour begins with a movie and a naturalist discussing the unique aspects of this species, especially its breeding habits. The warbler will nest only in young jack pine stands characterized by dense clumps of trees interspersed with numerous small, grassy openings. The pines must reach at least 5 feet (Christmas tree size), but not exceed 16 to 20 feet in height, when they begin dropping their lower branches. The bird nests on the ground where the lowest branches intertwine with grasses growing beneath the trees.

After the talk at the DNR or Forest Service office, the group drives into the Kirtland's Warbler Habitat Management Area, a 135,000-acre preserve of federal and state land, and the naturalist leads a hike through the jack pine in search of the bird. The hike ranges from 1 to 2 miles in length, with frequent stops to examine other birds, most notably the prairie warbler, upland sandpiper, and eastern bluebird, as well as other wildlife and plants. Spotting a Kirtland's warbler is not guaranteed but almost "virtually assured" during tours from late May through June.

27.
NEGWEGON
BEACH TRAIL
NEGWEGON STATE PARK

Activity: Day hike
County: Alcona
Difficulty: Moderate
Length: 4 miles one way
Fee: Vehicle entry fee
Information: Harrisville State Park, (517) 724-5126

■ Looking for adventure? Try driving to Negwegon State Park. The remote 1,800-acre state park is at the end of a rough dirt road often covered with mounds of drifting sand and sliced by the deep ruts of spinning tires. Developed facilities within the park are limited to a gravel parking lot and a water spigot—no campgrounds, no bathhouse, not even any vault toilets. Just 6.5 miles of beautiful and usually isolated sandy Lake Huron shoreline that is best seen from the park's 4-mile Beach Trail.

Someday this might change, as the park is gradually being developed by the state Department of Natural Resources. They might even grade the access road and add a campground, but hopefully the undeveloped beauty and unspoiled beaches of Negwegon will always remain. From Harrisville the park is reached by following US-23 north from 10.6 miles and then departing onto Fontaine Road for 1.6 miles. When Fontaine dead-ends, turn right onto Black River Road for 0.2 mile and then left onto Sand Hill Trail, the unmarked, rough access road which is very soft in some

Deer prints along the Beach Trail, Negwegon State Park

spots. Follow it for 2.6 miles to a wide gravel road that is posted with "Negwegon State Park" signs. Turn east (right) and reach the parking area in a mile.

The trail is level and dry and children can handle it easily in tennis shoes. Pack a bathing suit and some towels, along with a water bottle, as there are many opportunities in the first half to stop and enjoy a beach of your own. From the parking area, walk past the yellow gate and water spigot and look for the blue DNR pathway marker on a tree. The trail begins as a sandy, four-wheel track with paper birch on one side and a line of red pine and views of Lake Huron on the other.

At 0.6 mile you pass an obvious campsite beneath the pines where more than one person has pitched a tent on the soft carpeting of needles—with the door facing the lake, of course. The trail swings out of the pines and close to the shoreline at 0.9 mile, where there is a pathway marker, one of the few along the route. Take a moment to study the sandy area, as there will probably be more deer tracks than footprints.

After passing through a stand of paper birch and cross-

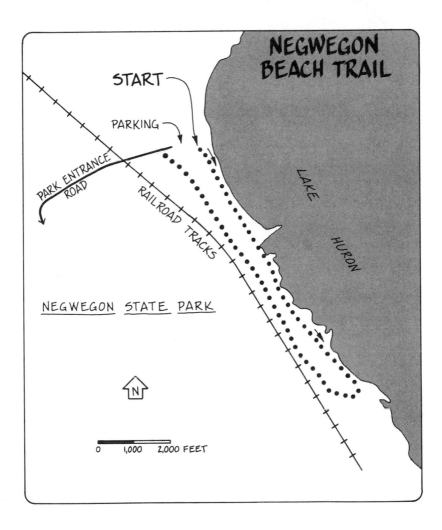

ing a small creek, you return to the edge of the pines along
the shoreline and follow a soft, sandy path while enjoying an
uninterrupted view of Lake Huron for the next 0.6 mile.
This ends at a marker at 1.8 miles as the trail begins to leave
the shoreline and swing into the forest. At 2.2 miles it takes a
sharp turn inland, crosses a bog area, and quickly emerges at
a railroad track.

The trail stays close to the tracks until the final mile,
where it veers to the east (right) and you enter the most enchanting paper birch stand of the day. This is the most scenic
section of the back stretch and on a clear day children will en-

joy the stroll through a forest of white trunks highlighted by patches of bright green leaves and set against a backdrop of deep blue sky. The forest gradually changes to aspen and oak and then at 4 miles you reach the bright yellow gate that closes the trail off to motorized vehicles from the parking area.

28. BELL TOWNSITE
BESSER NATURAL AREA

Activity: Day hike
County: Presque Isle
Difficulty: Easy
Length: 1 mile one way
Fee: None
Information: DNR Alpena office, (517) 354-2209

■ What could be more exciting than viewing a shipwreck? Hiking through a ghost town maybe? At Besser Natural Area it doesn't matter, for children are treated to both on the easy, mile-long hike through a rare stand of virgin pine.

Jesse Besser was an industrialist and founder of a massive concrete block corporation in Alpena, but in 1966 he gave to the people of Michigan a 135-acre tract of land on Lake Huron, containing a magnificent stand of virgin red and white pine that escaped the swinging axes of lumbermen in the 1800s. The preserve also contains more than a mile of Lake Huron shoreline, including a small cove with a wide, sandy beach lined by towering pines.

The somewhat remote natural area is a 20-minute drive north of Alpena and reached by departing US-23 east onto Raymond Road and following it 1.8 miles to the posted entrance. The trailhead is marked by a large display map with a small box containing descriptive brochures.

The trail is a path through the pines, carpeted in needles and easily hiked in tennis shoes. Within 0.3 mile it passes a small lagoon that at one time was part of Lake Huron and contains the shipwreck. The best way to see the vessel is to slip on a pair of polarized sunglasses and leave the trail to walk along the narrow, rocky strip that encloses the pond on the east side. From this side the ship is less than 4 feet from

Part of the "ghost town" of Bell seen in Besser Natural Area

shore; in the middle of the lagoon is what appears to be a mast.

The ship was headed to Bell, a lumbering and mill town located near here in the 1800s. At its heyday, the town had a population of more than 100 and contained several homes, a sawmill, saloon, store, and school. The most noticeable remains of this "ghost town" are the rock pier along Lake Huron (not visible from the trail), a towering stone chimney, and the collapsed walls of a building whose steel safe and icebox counter indicate it might have been the saloon.

The trail ends by winding through some of the oldest and largest white pine remaining in a state that was once covered by them. There are also some red and Norway pine along the path, all so stately and tall that young necks strain to see the arched boughs at the tops of them. Plan on 20 to 30 minutes to walk the trail or, better yet, make it an afternoon adventure by bringing lunch and swimsuits for enjoying the beach.

29.
SINKHOLES

MACKINAW STATE FOREST

Activity: Day hike
County: Presque Isle
Difficulty: Easy to moderate
Length: 2.4-mile loop
Fee: None
Information: DNR Onaway office, (517) 733-8775

Michigan's most visible karsts are the Sinkholes of Mackinaw State Forest. A karst is a limestone region of conical depressions called sinkholes, abrupt ridges, caverns, and underground streams—all of which make for an interesting hiking terrain. The Sinkholes Pathway is a 2.4-mile loop around five such depressions, some more than 100 feet deep. If that's too much in one day for a child, there's an 0.8-mile cutoff that allows you to view the steepest sinkholes.

The area is located 16 miles north of Atlanta or 8 miles south of Onaway along M-33. From the state highway turn east onto Tomahawk Lake Highway for 2.2 miles and then north on a dirt road posted "Shoepac Lake Campground." In a mile this road leads past the entrance of the rustic campground and then reaches a parking area within view of the lake, really a sinkhole whose underground drainage was completely sealed off by clay and silt deposits, allowing it to fill with water.

The trailhead is located across the dirt road. The pathway is not difficult but does require climbing a few long slopes. Boots are not required and most families hike the entire loop in less than 2 hours. From the display sign, the trail veers to the north (left) and immediately comes to the first and largest sinkhole. It's amazing how deep and steep the holes are—you can stand on the edge and view the tops of trees and pines growing along the sides.

The sinkholes formed because the bedrock in this area is limestone, which dissolves easily in winter. Underground streams created large circular caves in the limestone, which then collapsed under the overwhelming load of sand, clay, and broken rocks left behind by the last glacier 10,000 years ago. These are dry sinkholes, unlike Shoepac Lake, and at the beginning of the trail many worn paths descend to the bottoms of the holes. While it's a quick trip down, keep in mind it's a long climb back out, especially for children.

The trail skirts the edges of the first two holes, providing good views of this unusual geological formation, and then at 0.4 mile arrives at post number 2, the junction of the cutoff loop. Head south (right) to return to the parking area or east (straight ahead) to hike the entire pathway. If you continue east, you'll quickly skirt the third hole and then swing away to cross an area of scattered pines, the result of a 1939 forest fire. You pass a view of the fourth hole at 0.8 mile and then cut through more regenerating forest before coming to post number 3, marked with a "You Are Here" map.

At this point the trail swings south and makes a long ascent through a pine plantation to top off in a thick growth of aspen. Somewhere along the way there's supposed to be an

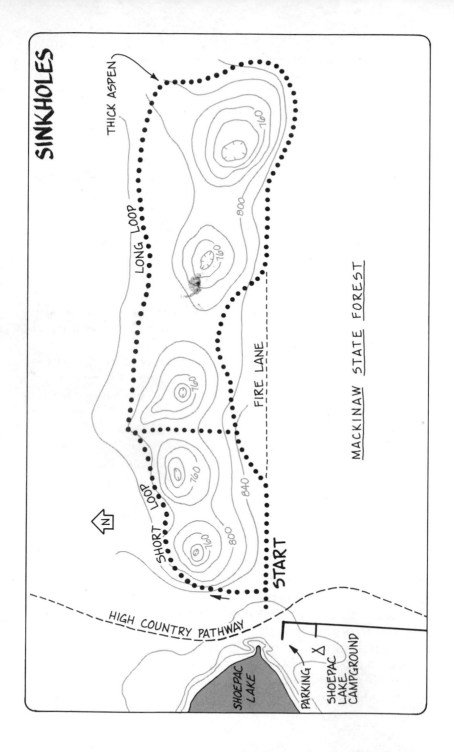

SINKHOLES

THICK ASPEN

LONG LOOP

SHORT LOOP

N

760

760

800

760

760

840

800

760

800

START

FIRE LANE

MACKINAW STATE FOREST

HIGH COUNTRY PATHWAY

SHOEPAC LAKE

PARKING

SHOEPAC LAKE CAMPGROUND

abandoned coyote den, but most hikers miss it, even the ones looking for it. At 1.3 miles the trail swings to the west to give way to the only view of the fifth sinkhole. You move from aspen to the jack pine that took root after the 1939 fire, and at 1.7 miles pass the edge of the fourth hole.

The trail swings inland at this point, but many parties unwittingly continue on the arrow-straight track, which is a fire lane. At 2 miles you reach post number 4, the junction with the cutoff loop, and then finish the hike by skirting the south side of the first two holes and viewing the sandy edge on the other side where you were hiking just an hour or two earlier. Throughout much of the last half mile of the pathway you can look down the straight trail and see the shimmering waters of Shoepac Lake. If the day is hot, it's hard to resist the temptation of dashing from the end of the pathway into the cooling waters of this most refreshing sinkhole.

▌30.
NEW PRESQUE ISLE
LIGHTHOUSE
PRESQUE ISLE TOWNSHIP LIGHTHOUSE PARK

Activity: Day hike
County: Presque Isle
Difficulty: Easy
Length: 1.3-mile loop
Fee: None
Information: Lighthouse caretaker, (517) 595-2059

▌ There's an old legend about the New Presque Isle Lighthouse (which really isn't so new at all—it was built in 1870). According to the folktale, the wife of one keeper could not cope with the long periods of isolation and loneliness and eventually went insane. The poor husband, not knowing what to do, simply locked her up in the cellar and then bricked her in. To this day, locals will tell you, with a sly grin and a shake of the head, that on the windy nights that fre-

New Presque Isle Lighthouse, the tallest lighthouse on the Great Lakes

quent the North Point of Presque Isle, you can still hear the woman moaning from her perpetual loneliness.

Lighthouses are always intriguing to children. But throw in a ghastly legend with a scenic but short day hike, a little freighter-watching, and a picnic at the end of a point, and it makes a great adventure for upstart hikers, even those as young as three. The 99-acre township park is reached from US-23, north of Alpena, by turning onto Grand Lake Road (also called Country Road 405). Follow the winding road through the town of Presque Isle, around Presque Isle Harbor, and past the old lighthouse, now a museum. The road ends at the park, which is open daily from 8:00 A.M. to 10:00 P.M.

Built to replace Old Presque Isle Lighthouse, the new tower is 109 feet high, making it the tallest lighthouse structurally on the Great Lakes. From the attached keeper's house, which is presently being restored as a museum, a spiral staircase of 144 steps leads to the light at the top of the tower. Still under the watchful eye of the Coast Guard, the lighthouse is closed to the public except when special guided tours are held during Fourth of July and Labor Day celebrations in the park.

The trail begins just north of the tower and is posted "North Bay Trail." This is a wide, wood-chip path that weaves among the hardwoods and pines for 0.3 mile until it arrives at the rocky shoreline of the bay. At this point a "North Point" sign points north along the shore. Children will soon learn that walking on large stones isn't nearly as easy as on wood chips, but luckily there are benches along the way and the view is pleasant.

Especially at the last bench near the tip of the point— there it's possible to watch lake freighters slowly making their way through Lake Huron. The point is reached after 0.5 mile along the shoreline and is marked by a large picnic pavilion and a tall directional post. The post points the direction of each of the twenty-one lighthouses along Lake Huron and a corresponding map attached to the pavilion shows the exact locations.

Across from the picnic shelters is the final leg of the hike, a wood-chip path posted "Nature Trail." The path stays in the forest away from the shoreline, but the last section is lined with scenic white paper birch. It ends within view of the lighthouse.

31.
OCQUEOC
FALLS
MACKINAW STATE FOREST

Activity: Day hike
County: Presque Isle
Difficulty: Moderate
Length: 3-mile loop
Fee: None
Information: Onaway DNR office, (517) 733-8775

■ While the Upper Peninsula has hundreds of waterfalls, the Lower Peninsula has only two, with Ocqueoc Falls being the most popular and accessible one south of the Mackinac Bridge. You can rush from the parking lot to the falls in a couple of minutes, but the best way to turn this stop into an adventure is first to hike a portion of the Ocqueoc Falls Pathway, a bicentennial project built in 1976. The trail is designed for both hiking and cross-country skiing, and consists of 3-, 5-, and 6-mile loops. It makes an excellent choice for children because the first and shortest loop is also the most scenic.

The trailhead is well posted on Ocqueoc Falls Road, which can be reached from Rogers City by following M-68 west for 11.5 miles. When the state highway curves sharply to the south, continue straight onto Ocqueoc Falls Road for a couple hundred yards to the entrance. Across the road from the trailhead is Ocqueoc Falls Campground, a rustic facility (hand pump, vault toilets) with many sites situated on a high bank overlooking the Ocqueoc River.

The trailhead is marked with a large display map and immediately you have a choice to make: left or right? By heading to the east (right) you will save the most scenic section of the hike for the second half and the falls for the end. But the first leg isn't without its views either.

You begin by passing through a red pine plantation along a wide, sandy path covered by needles. It stays close to M-68 at first, but quickly swings away, ascending a ridge until

Ocqueoc Falls, one of two natural waterfalls in the Lower Peninsula

at 0.5 mile it breaks out onto the edge, where you can look down into the river valley or across to the forested ridge bordering it on the other side. The first leg continues as a level walk along the ridge, but keep an eye out for the blue blazes on the trees to avoid wandering off on an old off-road-vehicle (ORV) trail. Just before post number 2, the trees open up briefly for the best overview of the river valley.

The junction is marked by a "You Are Here" map. To extend the hike to a 5-mile walk, you continue north (straight ahead) and follow the second loop. To stay on the first loop, head west (left), making a quick descent and coming to post number 5. Then turn south, cutting through a stump-riddled meadow and crossing a trickle of a creek in a low-lying area. From there blue blazes direct you to make a wide, ninety-degree turn west, where the trail descends right to the river-bank for the first time.

At this scenic spot (lunch maybe?) the river's current twists and turns five times as it flows through a horseshoe bend. The trail continues south along the riverbank for the next quarter mile and, if the day is hot, it's hard to resist jumping in right here. Tell your hikers a better pool awaits them. About halfway along the leg back to the parking area, the trail climbs a high bank above the river and soon you come to another overview, 20 feet above a U-shaped bend in the river.

There's something about a north woods stream gurgling past you that soothes the soul and washes the worries away. But you don't have to admire it too long from this spot because the trail follows the river from above for the next 0.5 mile in what has to be one of the most beautiful stretches of stream-side hiking in Michigan. Within a quarter mile of the end, the trail veers away from the Ocqueoc and comes to a V junction. The fork to the left goes to the trailhead and display map. The one to the right leads straight to the falls, where young hikers can sit in a pool and let the cascade gush over them after their "long hike."

Ahhhhh!

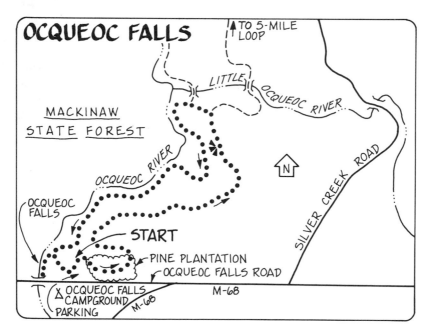

Opposite: *Nordhouse Dunes, the only federally designated wilderness in the Lower Peninsula*

LAKE MICHIGAN

32.
BACKROADS
BIKEWAYS
THREE OAKS SPOKES BICYCLE MUSEUM

Activities: Bicycling, interpretive center
County: Berrien
Difficulty: Moderate to challenging
Length: Loops of 8 to 60 miles
Fee: Bicycle rental fee
Information: Bicycle museum, (616) 756-3361

■ At the Three Oaks Spokes Bicycle Museum a velocipede is mounted on the wall. Built in 1860, this bicycle features two wheels, handlebars, pedals, a seat ... but no rims, rubber tires, or inner tubes. It was known, for obvious reasons, as the "Boneshaker."

Next to the velocipede is a classic Highwheeler from the 1880s; a little farther on you can view the beautiful, all wooden Huseby, an 1898 bicycle with handlebars made of elm and rims of hickory, all polished to a soft gleam. In all, almost a dozen bicycles are on display, everything from the Companion, a side-by-side two-seater, to the Recumbent, which, though it doesn't look like a bicycle at all, was used in the spring of 1986 to set a world cycling speed record of 65 miles an hour.

But the museum is much more than old bicycles and wall displays. What it's really showcasing is Berrien County, a pedlar's paradise locals call "Michiana." This southwest corner of Michigan, with its secondary roads, patchwork farmland, lakes, streams, and rolling hills, is a great place for a family bicycle tour.

The Three Oaks Spokes Bicycle Club set up the museum as the starting point and information center for its Backroads Bikeway, a selection of ten tours throughout the region, each posted with color-coded bike route signs. Situated on 110 North Elm Street in downtown Three Oaks, the center is open year-round from 9:00 A.M. until 5:00 P.M. daily.

Along with the bicycles that used to be and other historical displays, the museum has a video area with tapes on cycling and stacks of information, maps, and brochures describing the Backroads Bikeway and attractions along the routes. The club also rents bicycles for those who want to follow a portion of the bikeway. Not top-of-the-line ten-speeds, but definitely something a little newer and a little more comfortable than the Boneshaker.

The Forest Lawn Trail is best for children undertaking their first bike tour. Departing the museum to the south along Three Oaks Road, the 8-mile route follows a loop of Forest Lawn, Basswood, and Martin roads before returning to town. Along the way cyclists cross Spring Creek twice, pass three small lakes, and pedal through a landscape of pastures, orchards, and woodlands.

For older children, combining the 12-mile Elm Valley Trail with a hike in Warren Woods Natural Area (see 33. Warren Woods), makes an interesting day. The bikeway passes the entrance to the 200-acre state nature area where there are picnic tables, pit toilets, and a 2-mile trail through one of the only virgin stands of beech and maple forests in southern Michigan.

Another step up is the 30-mile Lake Michigan Trail, a good portion of which follows the rolling sand dunes and shoreline of the Great Lake. Other trails swing past cider mills, wineries, or Warren Dunes State Park. All end back at the museum where a quiet outside area with bicycle racks and picnic tables allows cyclists to rest their weary legs and enjoy a post-ride meal.

33. WARREN WOODS
WARREN WOODS NATURAL AREA

Activity: Day hike
County: Berrien
Difficulty: Easy
Length: 2-mile loop
Fee: Vehicle entry fee
Information: Warren Dunes State Park, (616) 426-4013

■ Most of Michigan's remaining stands of virgin timber are located either in the northern portion of the Lower Peninsula or in the Upper Peninsula. Except one. Surprisingly, in the southwest corner of the state, less than 10 miles from the Indiana border, are trees so big that most adults can't stretch their arms around the trunks and most children can't see the lofty tops. This unique spot is Warren Woods Natural Area, a 200-acre reserve featuring a rare, primeval beech and maple stand.

The trees were spared the logger's axe because Edward Warren, who owned a general store in Three Oaks, purchased the parcel to obtain the last surviving virgin hardwoods left in the state. A radical idea at the time—Warren purchased the woods in 1879, only seven years after the first national park and wildlife preserve in the country, Yellowstone National Park, was established. Today Warren's incredible foresight is well appreciated by anybody who hikes the area's 2-mile loop trail, which winds along the sluggish Galien River and past these impressive trees.

The park is open daily from 8:00 A.M. until dusk year-round, but the best time to come is late September through

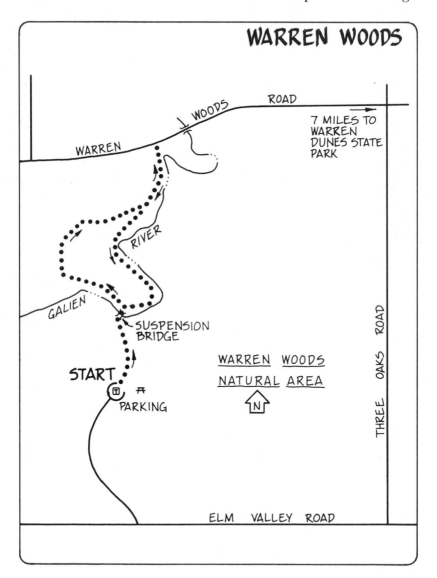

mid-November, when the leaves take on their autumn colors. The natural area can be reached from I-94 by departing at Union Pier (exit 6) and heading east on Elm Valley Road for 2.5 miles to an unmarked entrance. There is also a posted trailhead on Warren Woods Road, 7 miles east of Warren Dunes State Park, but the southern entrance is the best place to begin the hike. From Elm Valley Road it's a quarter-mile drive to a parking area with vault toilets, tables, and a large display map.

The trail begins as a wide, wood-chip path just east of the display, skirting a wooded ridge. The trees are nice but not overly impressive. Be patient. In 0.3 mile you come to a pair of benches situated on a bluff overlooking the Galien River and a wooden suspension bridge across it. Steps descend to the bridge and on the other side the trail splits. Head west (left) to have the blue DNR pathway triangles facing you. The trail follows the riverbank for a short spell, then ascends a high bank for an overview of the water. At 0.5 mile from the start, the trail takes a sharp swing north and enters for the first time the rare stand of virgin hardwoods.

If the size of the trees doesn't overwhelm children, explain to them that as far as the Department of Natural Resources can verify this portion of Warren Woods has never been deliberately disturbed by man. Loggers have not come through and practiced selective cutting; park officials have never removed fallen trees and deadwood. This is as natural as it gets in today's world. At 0.7 mile, you arrive at the junction with the return trail to the bridge. But don't skip the quarter mile to the trailhead at Warren Woods Road; that is where the largest trees are. It's almost mind-boggling that at one time all southern Michigan was covered by forest like this. One beech along the trail is so large that it takes two people to form a link around its trunk.

The return trail is a level walk following a ridge from the junction and in 0.2 mile it comes to a view of the Galien River, which most of the year, especially in the summer, is a slow-moving and muddy waterway. Eventually the trail descends the bluff, then hugs the riverbank for 0.3 mile before arriving at the bridge, which you cross to return to the parking area.

Hiker in Love Creek County Park

34.
LOVE
CREEK
LOVE CREEK COUNTY PARK

Activities: Snowshoeing, skiing
County: Berrien
Difficulty: Moderate
Length: 3 miles round-trip
Fee: Vehicle entry fee, snowshoe rental fee
Information: Love Creek Nature Center, (616) 471-2617

■ You can go nordic skiing at hundreds of places across Michigan, but for a change of pace slip on a pair of snowshoes and trudge your way up the hills and through the beech and maple climax forest at Love Creek County Park. The 100-acre facility features a variety of terrain, more than 5 miles of trails, and a nature center with exhibits and displays. Come winter the trails are groomed for skiing and snowshoeing and the interpretive building becomes a warming center and a place to rent equipment.

The park is east of Berrien Springs and can be reached from US-31/33 by crossing the St. Joseph River and turning east (left) on Pokagon Road. Follow Pokagon Road for 2 miles and then turn north (left) onto Huckleberry Road to reach the posted entrance in a mile. The park is open from dawn to dusk daily and the nature center from 10:00 A.M. to 5:00 P.M. Wednesday through Saturday, when a naturalist is on hand to explain the trail system and outfit your group in either skis or snowshoes.

Snowshoes are usually easier for children (and non-skiing parents) to master than skis because they don't require as much balance. As one naturalist put it, "Basically, all the kids have to learn is to pick up their feet." The rug-beaters can make for a fun and unusual adventure in the middle of the winter, when sufficient snow is on the ground (call the nature center ahead of time for snow conditions). Love Creek offers a range of sizes, but unless children are at least seven years old, their boots are usually too small for the bindings.

Fix everybody up with snowshoes, get a few tips for using them, and then head outside, where there might be a few initial spills until everyone gets used to their Donald Duck feet. The park has an extensive network of trails through its preserve, but trail number 11 is one of the most scenic walks anytime of the year. It's located at the west end of the park and makes for a 3-mile round-trip.

From the nature center depart along trail number 2, being careful not to step in the groomed ski tracks. This path cuts through an open field, so newcomers to snowshoeing won't have to negotiate trees or hills right away. In a quarter mile you arrive at the junction with trail number 10 and the start of the beech and maple forest. The 0.5-mile trail crosses Love Creek three times, descending sharply the second and third times into a ravine that has been dubbed Love Creek Valley. After the third crossing you climb out of the valley to the posted junction with trail number 11.

This mile-long loop winds through the climax forest of huge trees whose branches will be laden with a blanket of white after a fresh snowfall. Head west (left) and watch for deer tracks, which look like pear slices in the snow. In 0.5 mile the trail swings north and returns to Love Creek, skirting it from on top of the ravine. In another quarter mile you

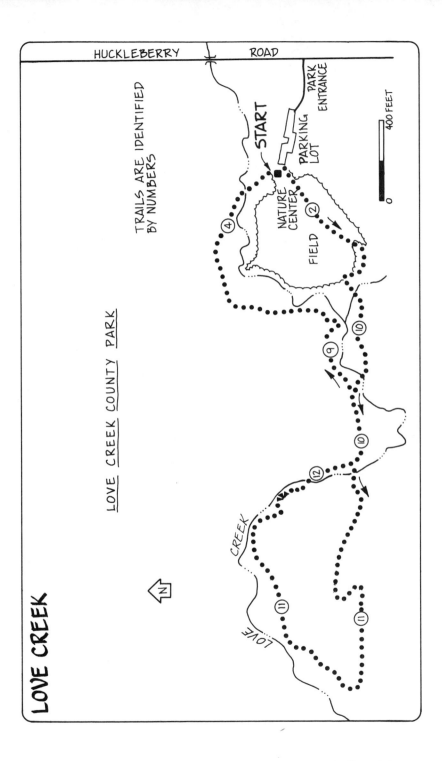

LOVE CREEK

HUCKLEBERRY ROAD

PARK ENTRANCE

START

PARKING LOT

NATURE CENTER

FIELD

TRAILS ARE IDENTIFIED BY NUMBERS

LOVE CREEK COUNTY PARK

N

LOVE CREEK

400 FEET

come to the junction of trail number 12, which you take south along the edge of the valley to arrive at a bench overlooking the frozen creek, perhaps the most scenic spot in the park and a good place to break open the thermos of hot chocolate.

The trail then dips into the valley and merges into number 10. You're still a mile from home, but to avoid backtracking follow trails number 9 and 4, which will keep you in the woods and cross Love Creek one more time just before emerging at the nature center.

35.
MICHIGAN FISHERIES INTERPRETIVE CENTER
WOLF LAKE STATE FISH HATCHERY

Activity: Interpretive center
County: Van Buren
Difficulty: Easy
Fee: None
Information: Interpretive center, (616) 668-3388

■ Not everybody likes to put a minnow or worm on a hook, but it seems we all like to fish. From the salmon troller in the Great Lakes and the fly fisherman on the Au Sable River to the youngster who takes a cane pole and can full of worms to a small farm pond, fishing is as natural in Michigan as surfing in Hawaii.

The Great Lakes state is blessed with an abundance of water and plenty of fish, so it was only natural that when the Department of Natural Resources expanded the Wolf Lake State Fish Hatchery near Kalamazoo in 1983, it spent an additional million dollars building the Michigan Fisheries Interpretive Center. Situated on M-43, 6 miles west of US-131, the center is open year-round, with summer hours 9:00 A.M. to 4:00 P.M. Wednesday through Saturday and noon to 5:00 P.M. on Sunday.

The center attempts to capture all aspects of the Michigan fishery, from commercial fishermen and the present stocking program to the anatomy of fish. But to the delight of children, the displays are devoted mostly to sport fishing. In the lobby is a wall with plaques of the state's record fish—sort of a fishermen's "wall" of fame—plus a display case of early fly fishing equipment and a historical Au Sable river boat hanging above it.

In an auditorium off to the side, an audio-visual program on the state's hatchery operations is shown throughout the day, but by far the most impressive part of the center is its "Michigan Room." The walk-through exhibit area begins with a series of habitat dioramas: cross-section models of the various types of water that can be fished in Michigan, from the Great Lakes to a trout stream. Each model shows the species that will be found, the habitat preferred by the species, and even the lures used by frustrated anglers trying to land one of the lunkers.

Beyond the dioramas are a series of hands-on exhibits explaining everything from the anatomy of a trout to the problem of the sea lamprey eel. The exhibits end with an area devoted to sport-fishing gear, including a delightful display of more than a hundred antique plugs and lures and a wall full of mounted Michigan fish.

From the center, troop down to the hatchery itself, where visitors are encouraged to view the operation and ask the staff questions. Most impressive are the ten concrete raceways outside the hatchery which can hold up to 120,000 pounds of fish at one time. The long tanks are labeled with whatever species is in them: salmon, steelhead, or walleye.

The most interesting fish, and easiest to identify, is the tiger muskie. The 6- to 8-inch muskies, with distinctive tiger stripes on their sides, are extremely active, darting back and forth, even taking small leaps completely out of the water.

The kids want to see something bigger?

Then ask for some fish feed at the interpretive center and walk out on the small pier of the visitor's pond. The small lake was developed so people, especially children, could actually see some large fish. It contains, among other species, a sturgeon that is 5 feet long and weighs 55 pounds.

Imagine that at the end of your line.

36.
MOUNT
BALDHEAD
MOUNT BALDHEAD AND OVAL BEACH RECREATION AREA

Activities: Day hike, ferry ride
County: Allegan
Difficulty: Moderate
Length: 1 to 1.8 miles round-trip
Fee: Ferry passage fee
Information: Peterson Steamship Company, (616) 857-2107

■ Saugatuck, that trendy resort town on Lake Michigan, is hardly wilderness, but it does offer a fun adventure that includes a ride on a hand-pulled chain ferry, climbing Mount Baldhead, and sweeping views from the top of the forested sand dune. It ends with a pleasant descent of the dune's west side to Oval Beach, Saugatuck's renowned stretch of sand and Lake Michigan surf.

View from Mount Baldhead on the trail to Oval Beach Recreation Area

The hike to the beach is short but does involve a stairway of 282 steps, a climb that leaves most people, parents and kids, puffing at the top. Benches have been built into the sides of the stairs, allowing you to take as much time and as many breaks as necessary to scale the "mountain." Pack along lunch or a snack, bathing suits, towel, and suntan lotion.

Saugatuck is south of Holland and reached by exiting onto Blue Star Highway (A-2) from I-96. Moored along the Kalamazoo River on the edge of the town's famed shopping district is an armada of cabin cruisers and sailboats 30, 40, and 50 or more feet in length. They arrive from home ports all over the Midwest and bob impressively in their slips during the summer tourist season.

A boardwalk paralleling Water Street winds past the luxury boats and ends at the most unusual vessel afloat—the Saugatuck Chain Ferry. The unique craft is at the foot of Mary and Water streets and is owned by the Peterson Steamship Company, which claims it is "the only hand-cranked chain-powered ferry on the Great Lakes," even though it only crosses the Kalamazoo River.

Saugatuck's chain ferry is a 150-year tradition. When the original one, a chain-pulled wooden barge, was put into service in 1838, it was a much heralded event. Before then, friends and farmers spent a half day traveling 10 miles inland to a bridge in New Richmond, just to reach Douglas, which was only 100 yards across the river.

The tradition stayed alive even after the Saugatuck-Douglas bridge was completed in the 1920s. In 1965, Peterson built the present ferry, a small barge with white gingerbread siding and a 380-foot chain to pull it through the water. The chain ferry operates daily from the second weekend in June through Labor Day, and the trip lasts a mere 15 to 20 minutes, delivering passengers just south of Mount Baldhead Park.

The park has picnic tables, restrooms, a pavilion, and a 282-step stairway that leads to the top of the 650-foot high sand dune. It's an invigorating climb to the top and the view is excellent. From observation decks you can see much of downtown Saugatuck, the boat traffic on the Kalamazoo River, even the S.S. *Keewatin,* the historic cruise liner docked in Douglas.

On the west side of the dune are three trails leading to Oval Beach. Thrill seekers choose the Beach Trail, a wild romp down a steep, sandy slope that is usually topped off by continuing across the beach and straight into the lake for a cooling dip. To the right is the posted Northwoods Trail, a 2,112-foot-long path along the dune's wooded north side. This route has the mildest descent and passes one observation point along the way.

But the most scenic path is the South Ridge Trail, which departs the top of the dune to the left. The 1,534-foot-long trail passes a handful of overlooks with views of Lake Michigan, Oval Beach, and Oxbow Lagoon to the north. The path makes a more rapid descent through a pine forest to emerge just south of the beach along the entrance drive.

37.
DUNE
OVERLOOK
P. J. HOFFMASTER STATE PARK

Activities: Interpretive center, scenic overlook
County: Muskegon
Difficulty: Easy to moderate
Fee: Vehicle entry fee
Information: Park headquarters, (616) 798-3711

■ You can view the most famous dunes in the Midwest all along the state's Lake Michigan shoreline, but the best place to teach children the significance of these mountains of sand is at P. J. Hoffmaster State Park on the outskirts of the city of Muskegon. An afternoon in the park with young children, even those under the age of five or six, can begin with a visit to Gillette Nature Center, to learn about the nature of dunes, and finish with a climb up to the Dune Overlook, for an impressive view of them. Older families can undertake one of several trails that depart from the center through the interior of the park to the beautiful beaches along the Great Lake.

The 1,043-acre state park is reached by heading south of Muskegon on US-31 and exiting at Pontaluna Road, where you head west for 3 miles to the park's entrance. Signs direct you toward the south end of the park road where the interpretive center is located. Gillette Nature Center (616-798-3573) is open Tuesday through Sunday from 9:00 A.M. to 6:00 P.M. during the summer, and 1:00 to 5:00 P.M. Tuesday through Friday and 10:00 A.M. to 5:00 P.M. Saturday and Sunday the rest of the year.

The center was built in 1976 as a Bicentennial project to serve as Michigan's sand dune interpretive area. The two-story building is in fact overshadowed by a huge, windblown dune that is best viewed from a glass wall on the west side. On one side of the lobby is an eighty-two-seat theater that uses a nine-projector, multi-image slide show to introduce visitors to the world of dunes and succession. On the other side is the center's exhibit hall, where a series of dioramas, graphics, and wildlife sound effects tells the story, "From a Grain of Sand," about the origin of the Great Lakes and dunes.

On the ground floor is a classroom with hands-on exhibits, as well as live seasonal displays of snakes, frogs, and other pond animals. Young children enjoy this section of the center as much as anything upstairs, for they have an opportunity to touch and rub samples of elk, raccoon, and red fox fur, among others. They can also peer through microscopes at slides of butterfly wings and shredded snake skins.

A lesson in sand dunes can be complete only with a view of them. From near the nature center several trails depart into the park's interior. One, the Dune Climb Stairway, ascends a wooden staircase of 165 steps. It's no easy stroll, but benches are positioned along the way for those hikers, young and old, who need to catch a breath. It ends at a viewing platform on top of the dune, 190 feet above the lake.

From the observation deck a panorama of Lake Michigan and its shoreline stretches before you, but, most of all, there are dunes almost every direction you look. Well forested or windblown, these steep hills of sand make up the majority of Hoffmaster's interior. Most visitors know they are viewing a portion of the world's most extensive set of freshwater dunes but don't realize these are among the youngest formations in Michigan, formed only 3,000 years ago and constantly changing in their appearance, size, and effect on the environment.

38. LUGE RUN
MUSKEGON WINTER SPORTS CENTER

Activities: Luge, skiing
County: Muskegon
Difficulty: Moderate
Length: Ski trail, 2.5-kilometer (4.0-mile) loop
Fee: Trail fee, vehicle entry permit
Information: Winter sports center, (616) 744-9629

■ At the Muskegon Winter Sports Center in Muskegon State Park, children and their parents slip on tennis shoes, strap on helmets, and try something new—barreling downhill feet first on a funny-looking sled called a luge. Beginners depart from the lowest entry ramp on the 600-meter luge track, but they still zip along the iced runway at speeds up to 12 to 15 miles an hour—while lying on their backs.

For kids, it's the most exciting 12 seconds they've ever had on a sled . . . in any position.

The sports center is in Muskegon State Park, with a parking lot and warming area situated in the park's rustic campground. The park is reached from US-31 by exiting west onto M-120 and following park signs to Scenic Drive. The center offers not only one of the few luge runs in North America but also 8 kilometers (12.8 miles) of lighted trail, the most extensive night-skiing network in the Midwest.

The luge track, the centerpiece of the complex, is basically a narrow, three-sided box that snakes its way down a steep hill. There are three entry ramps and from the top one experienced runners reach speeds of up to 55 miles an hour during a 35-second trip. But first-timers start off slowly by purchasing a beginner's package that includes an instructional clinic, insurance, and the use of a sled and helmet for as many as twenty-five runs that day from the lowest ramp.

The complex offers visitors, even children as young as five, a rare opportunity to try the Olympic sport most people have only seen on television. There are just four other luge tracks in North America—at Marquette, Michigan; Lake Placid, New York; Calgary, Alberta; and Anchorage, Alaska.

The ski trails form two loops, a 2.5-kilometer (4-mile) run on level terrain, ideal for families with children, and a 5-kilometer (12.9-mile) run through the hilly interior of the state park, for advanced skiers. Both loops wind through a scenic pine forest, are set with a track machine daily, and lit so skiers can enjoy the enchanting experience of "nordic nights."

Along with a log cabin warming center, the complex offers equipment rental and ski lessons. The luge and ski season runs from late December to early March. Open luge clinics are offered Thursday through Friday from 5:00 to 9:00 P.M. and Saturday and Sunday 2:00 to 9:00 P.M. The nordic trails are open from 3:00 to 10:00 P.M. Monday through Friday and 10:00 A.M. to 10:00 P.M. Saturday and Sunday.

39.
SILVER LAKE
SAND DUNES
SILVER LAKE STATE PARK

Activity: Day hike
County: Oceana
Difficulty: Moderate
Length: 3.6 miles round-trip
Fee: Vehicle entry fee
Information: Park headquarters, (616) 873-3083

■ For the boy or girl whose sandbox never has enough sand, there's the Silver Lake sand dunes, the mile-wide strip that separates the inland lake from Lake Michigan. This is heaven

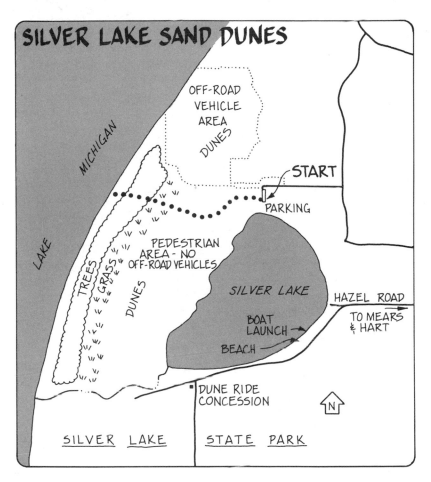

on earth for people who like to wiggle their toes in sand, climb steep slopes of sand, or run down dunes into a cool, refreshing lake. This, park rangers will say, is Michigan's own version of the Sahara Desert.

The 2,800-acre state park is south of Ludington and reached from US-31 by exiting at Shelby Road and heading west 6 miles to County Road B15 (16th Avenue). Head north for 5 miles, past the state park campground entrance, turn west (left) onto Hazel Road, and follow the "ORV Access Area" signs. This will lead you to the dune pedestrian parking area. Silver Lake sand dunes are divided into three areas. Off-road vehicle (ORV) users enjoy their motor sport in the north, a dune ride concession operates in the south.

Family returning from the dunes on the west side of Silver Lake

The middle is designated for hikers, who enter the area from a trail posted "Dune Access Stairway." From the top of the stairway, you quickly pass through an oak and maple stand and then climb a second set of steps to emerge at the open dunes of the park. The shifting sand is quite a sight. Towering ridges extend east to west in front of you; to the north you can hear and see the ORV riders in their own area. Any question about whether or not the sand is moving is quickly answered by a look at the trail sign at the top of the stairs—all but a few inches (post included) is now buried by a dune.

The hike out to Lake Michigan is a one-way walk of 1.8 miles, with several steep slopes to climb. Families with children under the age of six or seven might choose to walk to Silver Lake instead, by heading south (left) at the top of the steps along the edge of the trees. It's a 10- to 15-minute hike to where the steep dunes form the north shore of the lake.

To reach the Great Lake, select one of the ridges and begin scaling it. By climbing the one to the north (right) you will be able to watch the ORV daredevils racing along in a variety of vehicles: trucks with oversized tires, four-wheelers, VW "bugs," and homemade dune buggies. But the dune ridge straight ahead is visibly higher than those around it and its sandy peak rewards you with the best vista in the park, including views of both Lake Michigan and Silver Lake.

Here the sand is pure and sugarlike, and there's not a plant around, not even dune grass. After trudging along the crest of the dune, you descend to the section where grass has taken root. Technically this is a trailless area, but several routes are visible through the grass and lead into the strip of oak and spruce pine. Either put your trust into one of the routes or strike out on your own by just heading west.

It's about a 0.5-mile walk through the forest and then another short climb through windblown and grass-covered dunes before you reach the edge of a sandy bluff overlooking the Lake Michigan beach. What a beach! It is at least 30 yards wide and all sand, with the exception of an occasional piece of driftwood. The sand is smooth and almost white, the water is light blue, and there's often not another soul around.

40. BOWMAN LAKE
MANISTEE NATIONAL FOREST

Activities: Day hike, backpacking
County: Lake
Difficulty: Easy
Length: 2.2 miles round-trip
Fee: None
Information: Baldwin Ranger field office, (616) 745-4631

■ Unmarked from the road and hidden among the towering pines of the Manistee National Forest is Bowman Lake, a beautiful body of water surrounded by forested ridges and towering pines. The lake, really a glacial depression, lies in the southern end of the Bowman Lake Foot Travel Area, a 1,000-acre preserve for nonmotorized activities. The hilly

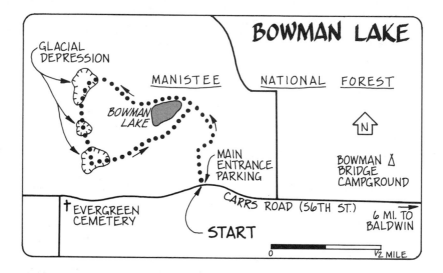

terrain is criss-crossed by unmarked paths as well as a portion of the North Country Recreation Trail. But circling the lake is a well-marked, 2.2-mile pathway that makes for a scenic but short day hike, ideal for hikers under the age of six.

You can spend 1 to 2 hours walking the path or pack in lunch, a rod and reel, and a can of worms and spend the afternoon fishing along the shoreline for panfish and bass. Bring a tent and sleeping bags and spend the night on a ridge above the lake, and chances are you might be the only ones watching the moon rise over the water.

The area is easy to reach but hard to spot from the road, probably the main reason for its light use during the summer. From Baldwin head west on Carrs Road, located just north of the Baldwin field office on M-37, for the Manistee National Forest. Continue on Carrs Road as it jogs left in 2.5 miles and then crosses the Pere Marquette River. The Bowman Bridge campground is on the other side, while the main entrance and parking area for the foot travel area is 1.5 miles farther west on Carrs (also labeled 56th Street). The trail is just a dirt road leading north, with a "Foot Travel Welcome" sign in the parking area. A second trailhead is another 0.5 mile farther west and if you pass the Evergreen Cemetery, you've gone too far.

Just north of the parking area is a well, while the trail, marked with blue diamonds, begins off to the east. The path

Fiddleheads pushing up through the ground, Bowman Lake Foot Travel Area

descends through a stand of pines and in 0.25 mile emerges at the edge of a swamp. Interesting place if the mosquitoes aren't too blood-thirsty. In May, the wetlands are filled with fiddleheads gently pushing their violinlike heads through the ground and organic debris. Later in the year it seems as though a million (zillion?) frogs are hightailing it into the swamp and children have to be reminded that frog hunts usually end with no quarry but wet shoes.

At this point there is a four-way junction with the trail east heading toward the Pere Marquette River, but it's often too muddy to hike in spring or early summer. You head west (left) toward the blue diamonds and in less than a 100 yards reach the east end of the lake. With the wooded hills around the body of clear water, Bowman Lake is a picturesque scene, though its muddy bottom makes swimming less than desirable.

The trail to the northwest (right) skirts the northern shore and then climbs away, and it doesn't take long to reach the first of three glacial depressions, marked by wooden pillars in the path. It's easy to imagine these large pits, devoid of trees in the middle, being carved out by glaciers 10,000 years ago. A blue diamond at the south end directs you across the open field, where you immediately climb into the second depression.

In the third depression a trail heads southwest to the other trailhead on Carrs Road. A blue diamond, though difficult to spot at times, is at the east end and directs you back into the trees. It's another half mile through the forest before you descend into view of the lake again, a happy moment for young hikers who might have been doubting your navigation ability. The trail skirts the south side of the lake before returning to the junction where you backtrack past the swamp to the parking area.

41.
NORDHOUSE
DUNES
MANISTEE NATIONAL FOREST

Activity: Backpacking
County: Mason
Difficulty: Moderate
Length: 3.9-mile loop
Fee: None
Information: Manistee District Ranger, (616) 723-2211

■ This is an excellent first backpacking trip for children, an adventure where they have to carry everything they need in their packs . . . or in dad's or mom's. The trails are wide and

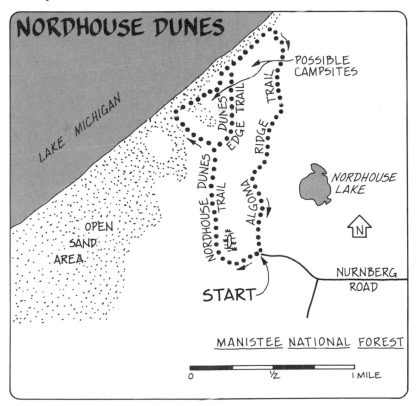

the days short. The scenery is unique, especially the open dunes along the lake. The wildlife is plentiful. But the most significant feature of the trip is at the beginning, while you're still in the parking lot. Posted there is a small brown sign, and if the children can't read the words then spell it out for them: "Forest Service Wilderness."

The Nordhouse Dunes, a 3,450-acre tract including a 4-mile shoreline along Lake Michigan, is the only federally designated wilderness in the Lower Peninsula. Young backpackers not only get an opportunity to experience an area where there are more deer prints in the dunes then footprints . . . but hopefully they will end the trip understanding why environmentalists fought so hard to protect the area from development. The value of wilderness is the most important lesson a family can learn from this adventure.

The trailhead is at the west end of Nurnberg Road. From US-31, head west (left) on Lake Michigan Recreation Road for 3 miles and then south (left) on Quarterline Road for a little over a mile to reach the junction of Nurnberg Road. There is little else at the trailhead except a parking area for your vehicle. Make sure you bring water with you. Three trails depart from this spot and it's best to start off with the Nordhouse Dunes Trail, the first leg of a 1.7-mile day. The path is at the south end of the parking area and is marked by a "No Motorized Vehicle" sign and a "You Are Here" map.

The trail is a wide sandy path that heads west and climbs slightly before skirting a pond and surrounding marsh area as it curves north within 0.3 mile. This is the first of several small wetlands and they are all excellent places to look for white-tailed deer and other wildlife, especially at dawn and dusk. Within a 0.5 mile you begin with a long ascent of a hill and follow it with an equally long but gentle descent on the other side of the forested dune.

At the bottom is a V junction with an old logging road, and in 1.1 miles you arrive at the junction with the Dunes Edge Trail, marked by a "You Are Here" map. To add a little more adventure, pass it up and stay on the left fork. This will lead you to a trail sign in 0.3 mile at the edge between the open dunes and the forested ones. The trail gets a little confusing here—this is, after all, a wilderness—but just swing in a northeasterly (right) direction as you follow along the edge of the lakeshore between the sand and the pines.

Soon you come to a wide band of open dunes and, faced with no trail signs, nor a really distinguishable trail, you cut across. This is great stuff, as far as kids are concerned, trudging across the soft hills of hot sand with backpacks on and Lake Michigan over their shoulders. You approach more wooded dunes and what appears to be a trail on the other side. Many parties camp here, others cross the next band of open sand that cuts inland until they reach a trail sign and the junction with one end of the Dunes Edge Trail. From there you continue along the Lake Michigan Trail as it ascends a wooded bluff and set up camp on top. Don't camp near the trail, while the open sand areas are probably the worst place to set up a tent.

Acres of open dunes lie to the south, waiting to be explored if you have a spare day. To return, you can either follow the Dunes Edge Trail and then backtrack along the Nordhouse Dunes Trail, or continue north along the Lake Michigan Trail, a hilly but very scenic walk, to the posted junction of the Algoma Ridge Trail. This trail heads inland to the south and in 1.7 miles returns to the parking area to make for a complete 3.9-mile loop.

42. MICHIGAN TRAIL
LAKE MICHIGAN RECREATION AREA

Activities: Camping, day hike
County: Manistee
Difficulty: Moderate
Length: 2.4-mile loop
Fee: Camping fee
Information: Manistee District Ranger, (616) 723-2211

■ To reach the Lake Michigan Recreation Area in Manistee National Forest you depart from US-31 onto Lake Michigan Road and then drive mile after mile after mile through an area of woods, wetlands, and much wildlife (especially deer), but few signs of people other than the cars you pass. Arriving at the campground, children feel they are in the middle of the wilderness—and they are.

The recreation area lies at the northern end of Nordhouse Dunes (see 41. Nordhouse Dunes), the only federally designated wilderness in the Lower Peninsula. It's an environmentally unique area that includes 4 miles of undeveloped Lake Michigan shoreline, 700 acres of open sand dunes, and 3,450 acres of wooded dunes. Upon arrival, kids jump out of the car and are overwhelmed by what they see: mounds and even mountains of sand, miles of open beach, and the inviting waters of the Great Lake.

This is paradise to them.

Situated almost halfway between Manistee and Ludington and 8 miles from US-31 at the end of Lake Michigan

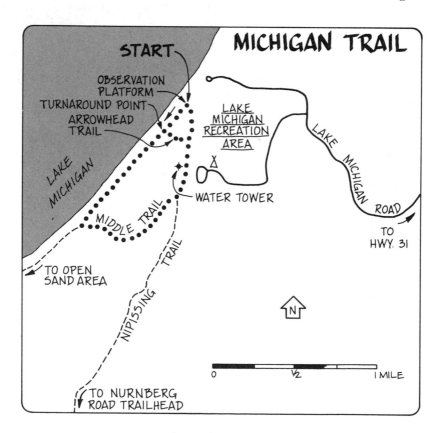

One of two observation decks that overlook Lake Michigan, Lake Michigan Recreation Area

Road, the recreation area features 100 rustic and wooded campsites well spaced along four loops. There are hand pumps for water, fire rings, and picnic tables, but no electricity or showers. The area is open year-round and managed from mid-May to mid-October. Advance reservations are possible for an additional fee by calling 1-800-283-2267.

There is much to do for families during the day: swimming, beachcombing, scrambling up the stairs of two observation platforms, and, of course, hiking, the best way to see the wilderness area. The campground is at the north end of a 10-mile network of trails through the Nordhouse Dunes, loops that range from as short as 0.8 mile to an all-day hike of 6 miles. But one of the best for children is a 2.4-mile loop that includes the first half of the Michigan Trail.

The hike begins with a scramble up the 122 steps of the southern observation platform, and if young hikers (or even mom and dad) can survive that, they shouldn't have too many problems with the rest of the route. The view was probably stunning at one time, but now it is partially blocked by tree tops. Right behind the platform is a red trail post and map sign indicating the Arrowhead Trail, the start of the network.

You can head either inland or toward Lake Michigan, but for most it's hard to pass up hiking along the shoreline first, one of the most scenic walks in the state. The trail actually follows a dune ridge high above the shoreline and is surprisingly level and easy walking. On one side of you are wooded hills, old dunes really, forested in hardwood, pine, and an occasional paper birch. On the other side is a steep drop, a strip of white sandy beach, and the blue horizon of Lake Michigan.

Within 0.3 mile of the platform you come to the junction of the Arrowhead Trail, the only cutoff point along the way. Head east (left) along the trail if anybody is having problems and you'll be back at the platform in 0.5 mile. The entire Arrowhead Loop is generally considered a 30-minute walk, even with young children. Continue south, however, for more of this enchanting walk along Lake Michigan and in 0.8 mile you pass through a scenic stand of paper birch and then arrive at the junction of the Middle Trail.

By continuing south along the lakeshore you will reach the open dunes but will end up hiking more than 6 miles by the end of the day. Head northeast at the well-marked junction, and you depart the lakeshore and head inland along the Middle Trail. Sure, you're leaving the lake and beach behind, but tell the younger members of the group that this is where you might spot a deer or even a couple of them, especially halfway along the spur when it passes a wetland area. Listen for crunching leaves and look for that white flag that always signals a sudden retreat of deer.

The Middle Trail is a 0.7-mile walk inland and ends at a junction with the Nipissing Trail. Head north and in 0.3 mile you pass a gray watertower that looks totally out of place. Take a break—you're now only 0.25 mile from the campsite. Continue north and the trail returns to the observation deck after passing two stairways, with the first leading down to the Oak Loop of the campground and the second to the Hemlock Loop.

Opposite: *One of many lakeside views along the Chain O' Lakes, Pere Marquette State Forest*

43. PLATTE PLAINS

SLEEPING BEAR DUNES NATIONAL LAKESHORE

Activity: Backpacking
County: Benzie
Difficulty: Easy to challenging
Length: Various loops of 3 to 6 miles
Fee: None
Information: Park headquarters, (616) 326-5134

■ Calling the Platte Plains area of Sleeping Bear Dunes National Lakeshore "plains" might be a little misleading. An aerial view of Platte Bay would clearly show the ancient shoreline sand dunes, which mark the successive positions of Lake Michigan after each intrusion of glacial ice melted. And

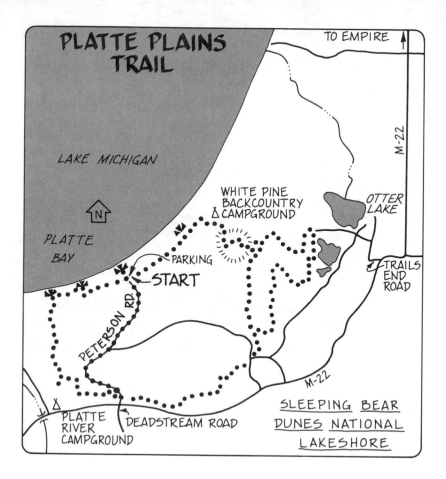

from an airplane, the dunes might appear as harmless ridges. From the trails, however, they're steep hills. And to a child, they're mountains to be climbed.

Not to worry. The beauty of the Platte Plains Hiking Trail, a 15-mile network of various loops, is that you have your choice of how to hike into White Pine Backcountry Campground. The longest loop is 6 miles, beginning from Platte River Campground, or you can choose a 5.6-mile loop that departs from a trailhead at the south end of Otter Lake. Both include a 0.8-mile stretch of steep, wooded dunes.

But if the children are young and new to the world of backpacking, Platte Plains can also be the destination for an easy and memorable experience of spending a night in Michigan's sand dune country. Part of the trail network follows old railroad grades and from Peterson Road it's a one-way walk of 1.5 miles into the isolated backcountry campground. Even children under the age of six can tackle this two-day adventure, since you backtrack to return to the car.

Begin the trip in Empire at the National Park Service headquarters on the corner of M-72 and M-22. Open from 9:00 A.M. to 7:00 P.M. daily, the visitor center has nautical and natural displays on the Sleeping Bear Dunes as well as information on other trails and activities and a three-dimensional map where kids and parents alike can see what they are about to climb. (You're kidding!) Pick up a free trail map to Platte Plans, or, if you want more detail, purchase the proper topographical quad. If you are planning to spend a night at White Pine Campground, obtain a backcountry permit.

From the headquarters head south on M-22. Within 5 miles you reach Trails End Road, which to the west is a dirt road that winds for a little over 1 mile around the south end of Otter Lake to a trailhead. This is the beginning of a 3.6-mile loop and by heading west (right) you come to a "You Are Here" map at the junction with the spur to the backcountry campground. The walk-in facility is another 0.8 mile away through a rugged area of steep hills—forested dunes, actually.

Continue another 3.5 miles along M-22 and you'll reach Platte River Campground, a rustic facility. A trailhead in the campground is the start of the 6-mile loop, which includes the rugged dunes and 2.1 miles of hiking along the level bed of an old railroad grade.

But the easiest entry begins at the end of Peterson Road, a dirt road located just north of the Platte River Campground, opposite Deadstream Road. Peterson winds 3 miles through the woods and ends at a parking area to a beautiful stretch of beach along Platte Bay. Hike 0.25 mile back up the road and look on either side for the posts with green directional triangles near the tops. The trail to the west (right, with your back to Lake Michigan) returns to Platte River Campground, a walk of 1.3 miles. To the east is the trail to the backcountry facility; it begins in a semiopen area along a sandy path.

Within 0.4 mile you move into a thicker forest of oak and pine, but the trail remains level, right to the posted junction of a scenic lookout to Lake Michigan, a mile from Peterson Road. The lookout is a scramble out of the woods and into the windblown dunes, where you can view the entire bay, as well as the famous Sleep Bear Dunes to the north and South Manitou Island in Lake Michigan. The trail leaves the junction and follows a gently rolling terrain that won't exert young children too much. Within 0.5 mile you reach the posted campground.

White Pine is located in a narrow ravine with wooded ridges running along both sides of the secluded sites. There's a vault toilet and community fire ring, but no water, so backpackers must carry in whatever they expect to use. With only six sites, this area is a quiet section of the park, even during the busiest weekends when other campgrounds are overflowing. There is no view of the lake, but from site number 6 a short path wanders west through the woods and opens into an area of windblown dunes. From the high perch of the dunes you are rewarded with an expansive view of the park's famous features, Sleeping Bear Dunes and South Manitou Island (see 47. South Manitou Island), while children will find the steep slopes of sand a tempting run.

Don't worry if they get sand in their hair during their mad dash down the dunes. Lake Michigan, with its clear waters and sandy bottom, is just a dune or two away. Return in the evening to sit on the last dune before the beach to watch the sun melt into Lake Michigan.

Observation platform along Pierce Stocking Drive, Sleeping Bear Dunes National Lakeshore

44.
PIERCE STOCKING DRIVE
SLEEPING BEAR DUNES NATIONAL LAKESHORE

Activities: Scenic drive, skiing
County: Leelanau
Difficulty: Easy
Length: 7.4-mile loop
Fee: None
Information: Park headquarters, (616) 326-5134

■ Pierce Stocking should see his road now. People are calling it the slowest, shortest, but most scenic stretch of pavement in the state. Pierce Stocking Scenic Drive in Sleeping Bear Dunes National Lakeshore is not long, a mere 7.4-mile loop, but mile-for-mile it has more breathtaking panoramas than most other roads in Michigan.

The road began as a dream of Pierce Stocking, a Michigan lumberman who also was a self-taught naturalist. Stocking had already built a number of logging trails in difficult terrain when he conceived the idea of a road that would loop along the top of the high dunes. Work began in the early 1960s and seven years later the road opened to the public. Stocking operated the road, charging $2 a car, until his death in 1976. The next year the National Park Service acquired the drive and eventually changed its name to honor the man who built it.

During the summer the road attracts a large number of cyclists, but its steep uphill and downhill grades make it a challenging tour. The best way for most children to experience the road is from the backseat of their family vehicle, with mom and dad stopping at every pull-off and overlook. This is a *slooooow* drive. Speed limit is 15 miles an hour, but even that at times seems too fast.

The posted entrance is 3 miles north of the National Park Service headquarters in Empire and is reached by heading northeast on M-22 and then turning north (left) onto M-109. The road is open for vehicles from May through mid-November from 9:00 A.M. until sunset and from a contact station at the entrance you can pick up an interpretive brochure. There are twelve numbered stops along the one-way road, where drivers can pull over to read the related material.

Stopping allows you to examine a variety of attractions, from a covered bridge that was once partially consumed by porcupines to a ridge that is appropriately named "Alligator Hill," to the intriguing aspects of dune ecology. But by far the most impressive pull-overs in Pierce Stocking Drive are the high vistas along Lake Michigan, scenic panoramas any season of the year.

Post number 3 is the Dune Overlook, with a wooden walkway and observation platforms at the end from which you can see the Manitou islands on the horizon, Glen Lake to the east, and dunes all around. Post number 9 is the Lake Michigan Overlook, and from a wooden deck you peer 450 feet down a steep dune to the Great Lake below. The adventurous with strong legs climb down to the shoreline (then back—definitely not recommended for children), looking like a line of ants from the deck. Post number 11 also provides a scenic vista of North Bar Lake, a former Lake Michigan bay that was impounded by a sand bar.

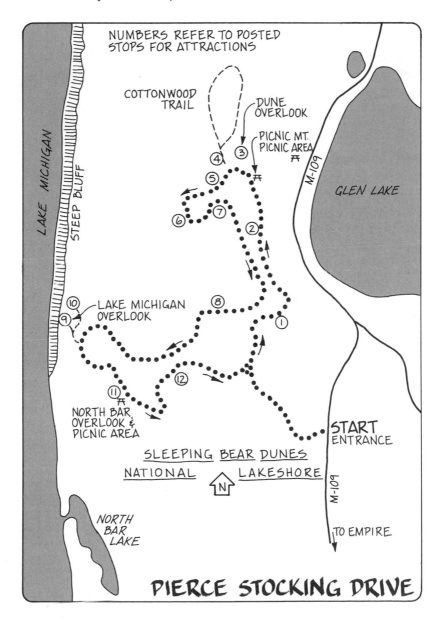

In between the pull-overs is Cottonwood Trail at post number 4, a 1.5-mile walk on the dunes that can be hiked by young children and provides a close look at the unique plant life and environment of dunes. The large picnic areas provided at the Dune and North Bar overlooks are so scenic people even savor their day-old bologna sandwiches.

The last few miles of the drive wind through beech and maple forest and an old pine plantation. Families with sharp eyes for details between the trees often make a stop here that isn't listed on the interpretive brochure—to watch for a variety of wildlife, especially white-tailed deer. Best bet for spotting deer is to be one of the first vehicles on the road in the morning.

WINTER USE

The loop is closed in mid-November but only for a few weeks. As soon as the first hard snowfall arrives, Pierce Stocking's road, one of Michigan's most scenic drives, becomes one of the state's most scenic cross-country ski runs. The road makes for a wide trail that can be skied in either direction and is rated for intermediate to advanced skiers.

45. DUNE CLIMB

SLEEPING BEAR DUNES NATIONAL LAKESHORE

Activity: Day hike
County: Leelanau
Difficulty: Easy to challenging
Length: Dunes Hiking Trail, 4 miles round-trip
Fee: None
Information: Park headquarters, (616) 326-5134

■ Sleeping Bear Dunes National Lakeshore is a diverse landscape that includes birch-lined streams, dense beech and maple forests, and rugged bluffs that rise 460 feet above

Running down the dunes at the Dune Climb, Sleeping Bear Dunes National Lakeshore

Lake Michigan. But the preserve administered by the National Park Service is best known for a 4-square-mile area of perched dunes on Sleeping Bear Plateau, and its famous Dune Climb, a 130-foot-high sand hill. Departing from the top of the hill is the Dunes Hiking Trail, the shortest and quickest route to reach the Lake Michigan shoreline.

The Dune Climb is fun for children of any age. Those under the age of four usually run out of energy halfway up the steep slope of sand and are either carried the rest of the way by a willing parent or begin the run downhill from there. Older members of the family can easily make it to the top of the dune in about 15 minutes, where they are rewarded with excellent views of Glen Lake to the east, Lake Michigan to the west, and Sleeping Bear Point to the north. The trail out to the Great Lake, however, is considerably more challenging. The round-trip hike takes 3 to 4 hours on foot and should be attempted only by children eight years or older who are in shape and have some previous day-hike experience.

Begin the day at the National Park Service Visitor Center, a nautical-looking building in Empire at the corner of M-22 and M-72, 22 miles west of Traverse City. The center is open 9:00 A.M. to 10:00 P.M. daily and features historical and nature exhibits, a slide program, and a wall full of free handouts about the park, including one on the Dunes Hiking Trail. From the visitor center head north on M-22, veer left onto M-119 and in about 6 miles you reach the Dune Climb.

The steep slope is only a few yards from the parking lot, store, and restrooms. Most visitors take off their shoes for the uphill climb in the warm sand and stop often to admire the view below or to watch others struggling up the dune. The top is marked by small stands of trees and a few benches that offer a shady place to sit and rest. The run down is exhilarating to say the least and often accomplished in a few minutes.

For those continuing on to Lake Michigan, remember that there is no water along the route and that the average hiker needs 30 to 40 minutes to cover a mile along the dunes. Fill a water bottle at the parking lot and pack along sunglasses, a hat, and sunscreen. Hiking boots or tennis shoes are necessary, as nobody should attempt this trail in bare feet.

The route begins with a hike up the 130-foot Dune Climb. Once on top, hikers strike out across the open rolling dunes, following blue-tipped brown posts that mark the 1.5-mile route to Lake Michigan. There are some stretches of gravel to cross, but for the most part this is an up-and-down hike across windswept dunes, which gently descend to Lake Michigan and a beautiful beach free of the crowds found elsewhere on the west side of the state. With children, plan on 1.5 to 2.0 hours to reach the beach and then follow the same route back to the Dune Climb parking lot.

46.
GOOD HARBOR BAY
SKI TRAIL
SLEEPING BEAR DUNES NATIONAL LAKESHORE

Activity: Skiing
County: Leelanau
Difficulty: Easy to moderate
Length: 2.8-mile loop
Fee: None
Information: Park headquarters, (616) 326-5134

■ The northern end of Sleeping Bear Dunes National Lakeshore on the mainland is Good Harbor Bay, the site of some small fore dunes, a scenic stretch of Lake Michigan shoreline, and during the winter, a cross-country ski loop that can be tackled by skiers of any ability. The 2.8-mile trail is maintained by the National Park Service, rated "easy," and is ideal for a child's first ski tour in the woods. The route is mostly flat, with only a few very short downhill runs that never exceed a ten-degree slope.

What is described as a wet and unappealing trail during the summer makes for a scenic and interesting ski run in the winter. The Good Harbor Bay Ski Trail begins near the frozen Lake Michigan shoreline before swinging into the pine forests where the region's heavy snowfall ladens every branch with a pile of white powder. Deer tracks are a common sight in the woods and occasionally a party of skiers will sight the animals themselves.

The trailhead is almost halfway between the towns of Glen Arbor and Leland along M-22, just about 9 miles from either one. Although not posted along the state road, the trailhead is reached by turning north onto Country Road 669 and following it to its end near the lakeshore. Turn west on Lake Michigan Road, which dead-ends at a small parking area and trailhead sign with an information box full of maps.

The trail follows a clockwise direction, heading east at the beginning as a narrow path leading into the pine forest. Quickly the trees thin out and you can hear and see Lake Michigan to the north. The best spot to cut across to the

Skiers returning from Lake Michigan shoreline on Good Harbor Bay Ski Trail

lakeshore is just before the trail curves south. Even if the bay is still open water, ice will be piled high along the shore, forming a gallery of interesting sculptures and shapes. If there is any wind at all, waves will be crashing into the jagged piles and creating eruptions of water and ice that explode high into the air every few seconds. It's an impressive sight in the stillness of the winter.

From the lakeshore the route turns inland and soon resembles an old logging trail. There are a few dips here and there, but no real "hills" that would overcome young skiers. After crossing a small bridge over a frozen creek, the trail passes a junction with another logging trail. This is the first of five such junctions, but green triangles always clearly point out the right direction.

The woods remain thick right to the end. Eventually you cross the same creek a second time as you curve to the north. After a good half mile, the trail swings west again, where the sound of waves crashing along the shoreline lets you know you are getting close to the trailhead and parking area.

47.
SOUTH MANITOU
ISLAND
SLEEPING BEAR DUNES NATIONAL LAKESHORE

Activity: Backpacking
County: Leelanau
Difficulty: Easy to moderate
Length: 2.4 miles round-trip
Fee: Ferry transport fee
Information: Park headquarters, (616) 326-5134 or Manitou
Island Transit, (616) 256-9061 or (616) 271-4217

■ Combining a scenic boat ride, the charm of Leland's
Fishtown, and beautiful beaches, South Manitou Island is
one of the best overnight camping adventures for children in
Michigan. Part of the Sleeping Bear Dunes National
Lakeshore, the 8-square-mile island has a fascinating natural
and human history, including a restored lighthouse, its own
set of sand dunes, and even a shipwreck that can be viewed
from shore. The island was the site of a farming community
and a life-saving station in the mid-1800s, but today the dirt
roads are footpaths and the only vehicles allowed on South
Manitou are those of the NPS rangers and a concessionaire
who offers a tour of the island.

The fun begins before you even set foot on the island.
You depart from Leland's quaint Fishtown, an old commercial fisherman's wharf whose docks and weather-beaten
buildings have been restored, giving this outing a sense of
"high seas" adventure for kids. From the end of the wharf a
Manitou Island Transit ferry departs for the island at 9:30
A.M., sailing daily June through August, and on Friday
through Monday plus Wednesday in May, September, and
October. The 1.5-hour boat ride is scenic and children find it
an exciting way to begin a trip. Bring suntan lotion, hat, bathing suit, and all your own food, as there are no supplies on
the island. When you arrive at the NPS dock and ranger station, pick up a map, a free backcountry permit, and register

for a site at one of three campgrounds: Popple, Bay, and Weather Station.

Weather Station is the best for children and the 1.2-mile one-way hike can be handled even by hikers as young as four or five. The trail is well posted and begins between the visitors center and the South Manitou Lighthouse. It's a walk in the woods, with most families stopping only to search for thimbleberries that ripen in late July and August. The trail finally breaks out along the high banks above Lake Michigan where the campground is located. There are some excellent camping sites here, overlooking a sandy beach below and Sleeping Bear Dunes off in distance on the other side of Manitou Passage.

Several activities can be sandwiched in before the ferry leaves the next day at 3:30 P.M., but a hike out to the battered wreck of the vessel, *Francisco Morazan*, will captivate children the most. It's roughly 1 mile from the campground to the sandy beach in the southwest corner of the island, where you

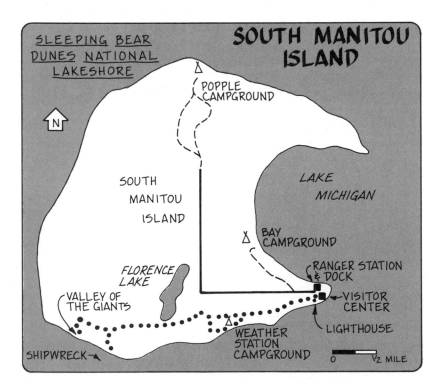

can view the freighter 200 yards offshore. The ship ran aground in 1960 and today almost half of it, midsection to stern, sits above the lake surface.

If the rest of your party is up to it, continue west for almost another mile to reach the Valley of the Giants, a grove of virgin white cedar trees and hardwoods. This is an impressive forest and one tree, identified by a small metal marker, is said to be the world record white cedar, measuring 17.6 feet in circumference and 90 feet in height. Even the wildflowers in this valley are huge, a good lesson for children about what Mother Nature can produce when left unmolested.

Don't pass up the excellent lighthouse program that ends with visitors climbing the spiral staircase for an impressive view from the top of the tower. For a brochure on South Manitou, write to Sleeping Bear Dunes National Lakeshore, P.O. Box 277, Empire, MI 49630.

Backpacker setting up camp at Weather Station Campground, South Manitou Island

48.
CHAIN
O' LAKES
PERE MARQUETTE STATE FOREST

Activities: Day hike, camping, skiing
County: Benzie
Difficulty: Easy to moderate
Length: Loops of 1.2 to 3.4 miles
Fee: Camping fee
Information: Platte River DNR office, (616) 325-4611

■ The old interpretive posts are nowhere to be found, but the Lake Ann Pathway in the Pere Marquette State Forest is still a scenic hike and a good choice for children. There are a lot of opportunities for shortening or extending this walk and plenty of places to stop for views of what many refer to as the Chain O' Lakes. The shortest loop is 1.2 miles, passing two lakes, an interesting bog, and a beautiful stand of pure white paper birch, and can be handled by children as young as three or four. The middle loop is a 2-mile trek that includes gazing down on the Platte River, and the long loop is 3.4 miles, reaching the edge of Tarnwood Lake and Platte River.

The trailhead is located in a Lake Ann State Forest Campground, a rustic facility of thirty sites, with many of them on a high, wooded bluff overlooking the water. The campground has a boat launch but no developed swimming area. From US-31, 18 miles southwest of Traverse City, turn north onto Lake Ann Road (County Road 665). It ends in the small town of Lake Ann, where you turn west onto Almira Road for 1.5 miles and then south a half mile onto Reynolds Road. The campground is posted from both Almira and Reynolds roads, and the trailhead is in a small parking area with a large display board and a registration box.

Blue pathway triangles mark the trail, which immediately crosses Reynolds Road and comes to a numbered post and map. By heading north (right) at post number 5, you'll skirt a bluff forested in maples and oak, spot Shavanaugh

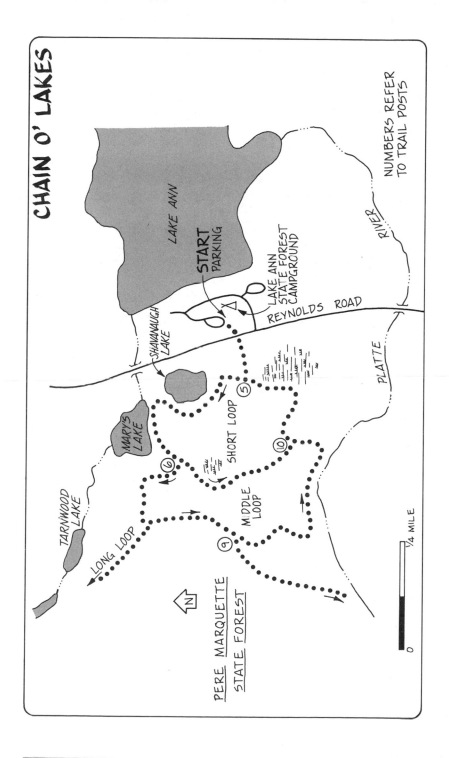

CHAIN O' LAKES

NUMBERS REFER
TO TRAIL POSTS

RIVER

PLATTE

LAKE ANN

START
PARKING

SHAVANAUGH
LAKE

LAKE ANN
STATE FOREST
CAMPGROUND

REYNOLDS ROAD

MARY'S
LAKE

TARNWOOD
LAKE

SHORT LOOP

MIDDLE
LOOP

LONG LOOP

⑤

⑩

⑥

⑨

N

PERE MARQUETTE
STATE FOREST

¼ MILE

0

Lake, and then drop down to the water at 0.4 mile. Legend has it that a man named Shavanaugh lived here in the 1800s and is now buried under "the big pine trees" on the opposite shore. The trail heads west and immediately skirts the southern shore of Mary's Lake, the next body of water in the chain. This is a beautiful lake, clear and free of weeds and framed by a white border of paper birch.

From Mary's Lake, the trail climbs through more paper birch before arriving at post number 6 and a bench. Head west to continue on the middle loop, which passes through a grove of white pine a century old and passes post numbers 7 and 9, the junctions to the long loop, in 0.5 mile. The trail heads south through a valley floor until you reach a low-lying area where the vegetation changes from maple and aspen forest to cedar (with the scaly bark), spruce, cattails, and dogwood. Shortly you will stand on a high bank with a bench and a partial view of the Platte River, which in 1966 became one of the first Michigan rivers to receive a planting of coho salmon, marking a whole new era for anglers in the Great Lakes. The trail skirts the river from above then swings north to post number 10.

The short loop, a 0.3-mile spur to post number 10, heads directly south from post 6 and quickly skirts a bluff above the most visible bog in the area, one with its center still an open area of marsh grasses. The trail doesn't drop down to the bog, but instead continues south to enter a natural forest opening where shrubs and plants play an important role in the survival of wildlife. Areas like this are the first to be free of snow cover in the spring. If it's August, take your time hiking in this and the other opening beyond post number 10—the area abounds in blackberry bushes!

After passing post number 10, the trail reenters the woods and passes a second bog, though this one is hard to identify because shrubs and trees have replaced the open area of marsh grasses. The trail skirts the bog from above and then ascends to post number 5, where you head east to return to the parking lot or your campsite.

WINTER USE

During the ski season, the pathway is set up with four main loops, including a 1.8-mile run on the east side of Reynolds Road that passes through the campground and is rated for novice skiers. The short loop on the west side of the road contains a few more hills but also can be handled by most novice skiers, while the middle and long loops are rated for intermediate to advanced skiers.

49. SAND LAKES
SAND LAKES QUIET AREA

Activity: Backpacking
County: Kalkaska/Grand Traverse
Difficulty: Easy to moderate
Length: Loops of 2.5 to 7.2 miles
Fee: None
Information: DNR Kalkaska office, (616) 258-2711

My father remembers Sand Lakes. In the 1930s, his uncle and aunt would pile him into an old Ford, along with a picnic lunch of cold fried chicken, and head south from their summer place in Elk Rapids, past Williamsburg to where the road ended. Here they followed old logging trails that were little more than two sandy ruts to the group of five small lakes. They would fish, swim, or just enjoy their meal in the quiet setting that the area offered.

Little has changed since then. The red pine are taller, you now have to hike in instead of drive, and a thick undergrowth of ferns has turned some of the logging roads into footpaths. But parents still arrive with their children to show them what a world without vehicles, motors, and man-made noise is like. You come to listen to the quiet.

Designated in 1973 by the Department of Natural Resources, the Sand Lakes Quiet Area is a 2,500-acre preserve of rolling forested hills, interspersed with twelve lakes and ponds and connected to one another by a 12-mile network of

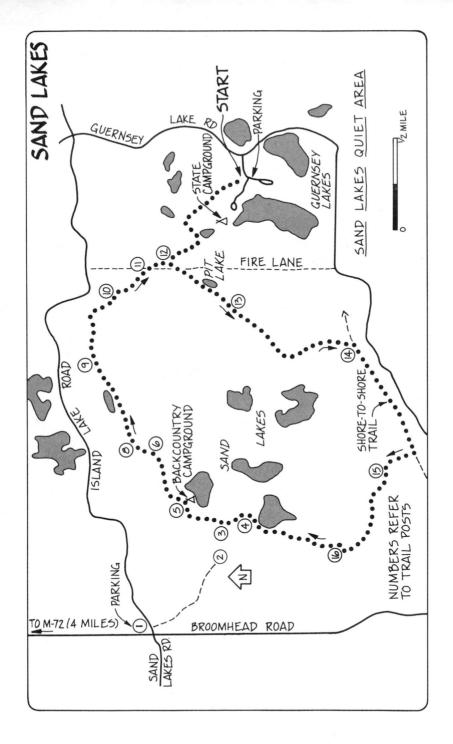

SAND LAKES

START

GUERNSEY LAKE RD

PARKING

SAND LAKES QUIET AREA

½ MILE

0

STATE CAMPGROUND

GUERNSEY LAKES

12

11

FIRE LANE

PIT LAKE

10

13

9

14

ISLAND LAKE ROAD

8   6

BACKCOUNTRY CAMPGROUND

SAND   LAKES

SHORE-TO-SHORE TRAIL

5

15

3   4

NUMBERS REFER TO TRAIL POSTS

2

16

N

PARKING

TO M-72 (4 MILES)

1

BROOMHEAD ROAD

SAND LAKES RD

trails and old logging roads. For the most part the trails form a 7.2-mile loop beginning at Guernsey Lake State Forest Campground with a backcountry campground located almost halfway on the edge of Sand Lake number 1, making it an excellent backpacking opportunity for children six to eight. The trails are wide, well marked with "You Are Here" maps, and, for the most part, easy to follow.

Even children younger than six can enjoy an overnight trip by beginning at a trailhead at the corner of Sand Lakes Road and Broomhead Road, 4 miles south of M-72 after departing on Cook Road. From there the hike from post number 1 to 2, 3, and finally 5, site of the walk-in campsite, is a one-way trek of 1.2 miles.

Guernsey Lake can be reached from Kalkaska by heading west from M-72 on Island Lake Road for 8 miles and then turning south on Guernsey Lake Road to the posted state forest campground. The rustic facility has twenty-six sites, including many that overlook the lake from a high bank, and a boat launch. Just before entering the campground, you pass a parking area on the entrance drive, with a trailhead and map box across from it. This trail is a forested spur to post number 12 on the main loop. Along the way you pass the northern arm of Guernsey Lake (appears as a pond on some maps) and in 0.7 mile come to the junction.

The shortest route to the backcountry campsite is the 2-mile northern half of the loop, while the trail leading south, a wide path through a forest of pines, oaks, and maple, reaches Sand Lake number 1 in 3.7 miles. Heading south, you soon come to a fire lane that veers off to the left and then Pit Lake, a small, round body of water, not on many maps. Are fish in there? Hmmmmm, maybe we should take a break. . . .

From the lake the trail heads straight for post number 13 and then continues south to post number 14. Along the way you pass unmarked trails to Sand Lake number 5, which might be a little confusing, but the main loop will be marked with blue blazes on the trees. At post number 14 you swing west and join a segment of Michigan's Shore-to-Shore Trail, a 203-mile, horse- and footpath that crosses the state from Empire on Lake Michigan to Tawas on Lake Huron. You actually skirt the Scenic Drive from above, though you rarely see the road, then descend to it at a well-posted junction. Head north and you quickly reach post number 15.

The trail returns to an old logging road and eventually descends to an open area of tall shrubs and saplings. A good area to look for deer, especially if it's near dusk. If you can't find the animals themselves, search the sandy path and you're sure to spot their tracks criss-crossing in every direction. At post number 16 the main loop swings to the north and continues following the logging road for 0.2 mile. But at one point the old road ascends a ridge forested on top and the loop, poorly marked here, veers off to the left.

You skirt a bog area, reenter the woods, and then emerge at Sand Lake number 3, a clear body of water where occasionally an angler will hike in to fish for bass. The trail skirts the lake and then arrives at post number 4. With the campground only a short walk away, just beyond post number 5, the first day is almost over. The facility is on the edge of Sand Lake number 1 and has a pair of vault toilets, a table, and a water pump near the lake. It's a shady, and very quiet, area with enough space for a half dozen tents.

The trail to post number 6 is a 0.5-mile walk that ascends quickly to post number 8 and then swings east toward post number 9. Along the way the trail skirts another small, unnamed lake where on a still evening you can watch the panfish rise and snatch bugs off the surface. Mushrooms in an assortment of colors grow in profusion along this stretch. The trail to post number 10 returns to looking like a footpath through the woods as it weaves its way through the gently rolling terrain. This is perhaps the most enjoyable stretch of the loop, but it ends all too soon as you arrive at the "You Are Here" marker and return to following the wide logging road. At this point you are only a mile away from your vehicle, via post numbers 11 and 12, and the spur to the state forest campground.

50.
SKEGEMOG
SWAMP
SKEGEMOG LAKE WILDLIFE AREA

Activity: Day hike
County: Kalkaska
Difficulty: Easy
Length: 2 miles round-trip
Fee: None
Information: DNR Kalkaska office, (616) 258-2711

■ One of the most scenic swamps in Michigan, with one of the driest trails to it, is located in the Skegemog Lake Wildlife Area, a preserve of 1,300 acres that was saved from developers by the Michigan Chapter of The Nature Conservancy working with the Department of Natural Resources. There are several viewing points of this sensitive area, including Skegemog Overlook, a roadside park on M-72 8 miles west of Kalaska, where you can enjoy lunch while viewing the lake.

But for the best view of the wetlands that border the lake, hike the Skegemog Swamp Pathway, an easy 1-mile walk out to an observation tower. The trailhead is reached by departing M-72 onto County Road 597 toward Rapid City. Within 4 miles you will see the posted trailhead and parking area to the path. The pathway is an interesting adventure anytime of the year, but bring bug repellent in the summer, and binoculars during the spring and fall, to watch the migrating waterfowl and other birdlife.

From the parking lot, you enter a predominately beech forest, carpeted in ferns, and then arrive at a former railroad grade. Trail markers direct you south along the old railroad bed for 0.5 mile to a trail sign and bridge leading into the woods.

The woods are lush and green. The trees are primarily cedar, spruce, and tamarack, which grow well in bog conditions, and the forest floor is carpeted in moss, wintergreen, mushrooms, and wildflowers. Jack-in-the-pulpit, with its white flower in the green pulpit, is one of the easiest flowers

Observation tower and boardwalk at the end of the trail through Skegemog Swamp

for children to recognize. There are also Canada mayflower, grass of Parnassus with its flower of five white petals, and great blue lobelia, with its delicate bluish-purple flowers. Study the display board at the trailhead, which has drawings of the various plants.

The trail follows a stream through the woods and consists of a boardwalk with scattered benches much of the way. Toward the end you cross the stream on a bridge and shortly emerge into the open area of cattails and march grasses, with the observation tower at the end of the boardwalk, 0.5 mile from the railroad grade. The tower is 16 feet high and provides a sweeping panorama of Skegemog Swamp, a maze of open water channels, and patches of cattails and other shrubs. On the horizon is the edge of the lake and with the aid of binoculars you can often spot a variety of birdlife, including Canada geese, great blue heron, a variety of waterfowl, and, if you're lucky, a bald eagle or osprey.

51.
AU SABLE RIVER
FOOT TRAIL
HARTWICK PINES STATE PARK

Activity: Day hike
County: Crawford
Difficulty: Moderate
Length: 3-mile loop
Fee: Vehicle entry fee
Information: Park headquarters, (517) 348-7068

■ The best-known foot trail in Hartwick Pines State Park is the Pines Loop, a mile-long path through the park's interpretive area that includes virgin white pines, a reconstructed logger's camp, and a museum dedicated to Michigan's lumbering era. It's a fascinating look at lumberjacks and shouldn't be missed during a visit to the area. But for a quieter, less crowded and certainly more intimate look at nature,

Footbridge over the East Branch of the Au Sable River along the Au Sable River Foot Trail

lead your children along the Au Sable River Foot Trail on the west side of M-93.

The 3-mile trail features two crossings of the East Branch of the Au Sable River, stands of virgin timber, and thirteen interpretive posts which correspond to descriptions in a brochure available at the park headquarters or contact station. A little bit of climbing is involved and a few wet spots must be crossed, but overall the trail is not difficult and provides a 2-hour escape from the often busy portion of the park.

Hartwick Pines is 9 miles north of Grayling and reached from I-75 by departing at exit 259. Head north on M-93 for 3 miles and at the park entrance turn east (right) toward the headquarters. The trailhead is posted along Scenic Trail just past the entrance to the DNR office.

The trail is marked with deer tracks, both on posts erected by the park staff and in the trail, left by the animals

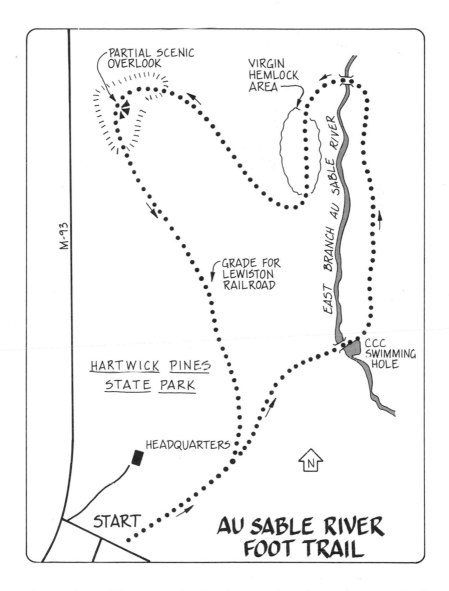

PARTIAL SCENIC
OVERLOOK

VIRGIN
HEMLOCK
AREA

M-93

EAST BRANCH AU SABLE RIVER

GRADE FOR
LEWISTON
RAILROAD

HARTWICK PINES
STATE PARK

CCC
SWIMMING
HOLE

HEADQUARTERS

N

START

AU SABLE RIVER
FOOT TRAIL

themselves. The route begins by passing through a stand of pines to reach the junction with the return loop, and then crosses an old vehicle track in 0.4 mile. In another 0.25 mile you reach the East Branch for the first time, where interpretive post numbers 2, 3, and 4 are clustered. There is a bench here and if you sit quietly long enough you might see the rings of rising trout forming and then dissolving in the stream's current. Post number 4 marks an old swimming hole, built during the 1930s by the CCC (Civilian Conservation Core) as a place for them to cool off after long days of planting pine saplings. Trout fingerlings can often be seen darting around its still waters.

The trail moves through a mixed forest of white, red, and jack pine intermixed with maple, balsam, and paper birch, and at 1.3 miles you reach the second bridge over the East Branch. The trail might get a little wet on the other side and post number 7 explains the reason: you're in a cedar swamp. The best stand of trees, however, is an area of virgin hemlock at 1.7 miles. The huge pines tower above the trail, making most children pause to study their grandeur and the shafts of light filtering down between them.

The relatively level walk turns into a climb when you begin walking up a glacial moraine to reach post number 11 at 1,240 feet. The scenic overlook described in the brochure has been significantly reduced by a growth of saplings, but some glimpses of the ridge line 4 miles away are still possible, especially if some members of your hiking party sit on your shoulders. After a descent from the ridge, the final leg of the trail is a level walk past a railroad grade of the Lewiston Railroad and a rectangular mound that many believe was once a barn.

52. FORBUSH CORNERS
FORBUSH CORNERS SKI CENTER

Activity: Ski
County: Crawford
Difficulty: Easy to moderate
Length: Various trail lengths
Fee: Trail fee
Information: Ski center, (517) 348-5989 or (517) 385-5411

■ There's always a pot of chili on at Forbush Corners.

The ski center, with its groomed trails, skating lanes, and inexpensive bunkroom accommodations, attracts advanced skiers from throughout Michigan and the Midwest, interested in training and improving their racing techniques. Bordering the northern boundary of Hartwick Pines State Park, Forbush Corners features 24 kilometers of trails, groomed and tracked for both skating and traditional striding. The network also connects with the state park's 16-kilometer (25.7-mile) system, making it possible for skiers to enjoy a 20-kilometer (32.2-mile) day through the woods without backtracking.

But for families, Forbush Corners is a friendly place that caters as much to children and novice skiers as it does to racers. There are always skiers relaxing in the two warming areas and a pot of chili steaming in the lodge kitchen. Rental equipment is available, as are single-party ski lessons, while trails rated "easy" or "moderate" feature some challenging side loops, making them ideal for a family of various skiing abilities.

THE GREEN TRAIL

This 3.5-kilometer (5.6-mile) loop is rated "easy" and winds through a mixture of open and wooded terrain. A few small hills are encountered, but overall the run is ideal for novice skiers and young children. Departing from it are several optional trails for the experienced skiers in the party, with steep downhill runs and equally challenging climbs, including one labeled "Lil' Stinker."

THE PINES LOOP

The longest trail at Forbush is the Pines Loop, a 10.5-kilometer (16.9-mile) run that extends into Hartwick Pines State Park. The run is rated "more difficult," as it features several long slopes that can be handled by families and older children with a season or two of skiing experience. The trail is a scenic ski both through stands of towering pines and through open terrain, with an option to go farther into the state park.

The Pines Loop begins behind the warming area and extends south into the state park, passing historic "Devil's Elbow," a posted hill that used to befuddle the lumberman's log sleds of the 1800s. Today the downhill run is considerably easier. After 5.5 kilometers (8.8 miles), the loop swings north to return to the ski center and enters the most scenic section in the final 3 kilometers (4.8 miles). Here skiers follow a ridge with a view of the wooded ravines on both sides. Near the end, advanced skiers have the option of swinging onto the Roller Coaster Trail, rated "most difficult," for some exciting downhill runs, including one labeled "The Corkscrew."

■ 53.
DEADMANS
HILL
MACKINAW STATE FOREST

Activities: Day hike, backpacking
County: Antrim
Difficulty: Moderate
Length: 3-mile loop
Fee: None
Information: Gaylord DNR office, (517) 732-3541

■ Begin this hike with the story about Stanley Graczyk. The twenty-one-year-old was a fun-loving lumberjack back in the early 1900s, known as "Big Sam" to his friends and fellow loggers. On May 20, 1910, Big Sam was to marry his child-hood sweetheart. That day, Sam's crew was working the steep ridges of Jordan River Valley, with Big Sam himself driving a team of horses and a "Big Wheel" loaded with timber down the ridge. Poor Stanley never even made it to the altar. The huge cart slipped out of control and ran over him, killing him instantly. It's been called Deadmans Hill ever since.

Today it's a scenic spot with views of much of the Jordan River watershed, and an especially popular destination during the height of fall colors. But the top of Deadmans Hill also serves as the trailhead for the Jordan River Pathway, a 2-day backpacking trip of 18.7 miles, and the Deadmans Hill Loop, a 3-mile day hike that combines a walk in the woods with a little bit of logging lore. The short loop includes a downhill section in the beginning and some uphill walking at the end, but the trail is wide, easy to follow, and a hike that can be accomplished in a pair of sturdy tennis shoes.

The walk begins and ends on top of Deadmans Hill, located off US-131 11.5 miles north of Mancelona or 6 miles from the hamlet of Alba. From US-131 turn west onto Deadmans Hill Road and drive 2 miles to the parking area and trailhead at the end. Before arriving at the trailhead, fill up your water bottles. There are vault toilets at the overlook but no drinking water. The trailhead is off the northern loop of Deadmans Hill Road and marked by a large trail sign and a box to leave your plans.

From the spectacular views on top of the ridge, you begin the trip by dropping quickly into the valley. The long descent to the valley floor lasts 0.6 mile, but along the way you pass several tree identification signs. The first is one rarely seen in Michigan; it points out an elm tree that somehow sur-

Observation platform along the Jordan River Pathway

vived the spread of Dutch elm disease in the 1960s. The trail bottoms out in an open area where it takes a sharp 180-degree swing to the south.

You reenter the woods, skirt a bluff, and within a mile come to post number 4, the river study area. An observation deck leads out over a feeder creek of the Jordan River, but unfortunately the interpretive plaques have been destroyed. The trail continues as a fine line between the base of Deadmans Hill and the wet low-lying areas around the river. You never actually see the river from the trail, but the ridge is constantly towering over you for an unusual walk.

Post number 5 is reached at 1.4 miles and here day hikers swing south while backpackers continue west. The cutoff spur first moves through an open area where sandy soil supports a healthy crop of wild berries. If it's early to midsummer, have the children search low to the ground for strawberries. If it's midsummer, then it's raspberries you're after, and in mid- to late August, blackberries will appear.

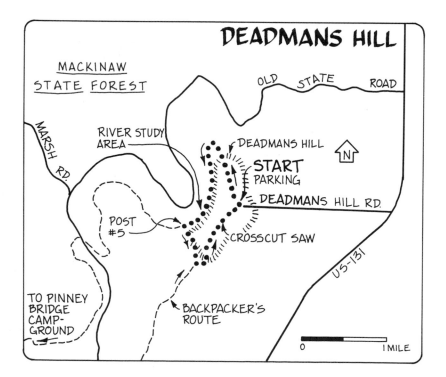

This portion of the trail might take you a while to get through. It's hard for a young hiker to pass up a ripe berry.

Eventually the trail reenters a young forest and begins a steady climb. Just when young legs are ready to give out, you top off at a posted junction. The trail from the west is the return of the backpacker's route, while the one to the east is the path to the parking area. The walk is an easy 1.1 miles from here to the end, with only a slight climb now or then. Just before you arrive at the entrance drive, look to the left side of the trail for the maple tree with a saw embedded in it. A sawyer broke his crosscut saw some fifty years ago and put both pieces in the crotch of the tree. The maple continued to grow, encasing the blades, one of which is still visible.

BACKPACKING

The entire Jordan River Pathway makes for a unique overnight trip which gives hikers an opportunity to encounter several active beaver ponds and other wildlife and spend an evening in the solitude of a backpacker's campground. Pinney Bridge Hike-in Campground marks the halfway point of the 18.7-mile trip, while along the pathway are numbered posts that correspond to a brochure's descriptions of historic and natural features of the area.

The trek is not an extremely strenuous hike and the steepest sections occur at the beginning and end, when backpackers are in the best frame of mind to endure them. But the trip does involve a 9- and 10-mile day, as well as climbing over several hills. Children under the age of seven or eight may have a difficult time walking the entire trail, and everybody, parents and kids alike, should have previous day-hike and camping experience and be reasonably fit before tackling the adventure.

Water is available from a pump at the hike-in campground and the second day at a state fish hatchery that lies a half mile off the trail. There is a two-night maximum stay and a volunteer fee payment system at the campground. No camping is allowed along the pathway other than at the Pinney Bridge facility. To obtain an interpretive brochure before the trip, write to Forest Management Division, P.O. Box 667, Gaylord, MI 49735.

54.
PETOSKEY
STONES
FISHERMAN'S ISLAND STATE PARK

Activities: Beachcombing, camping
County: Charlevoix
Difficulty: Easy
Length: Varying
Fee: Vehicle entry fee
Information: Park headquarters, (616) 547-6641

■ Children love dinosaurs and while it's tough to find any remains of a brontosaurus or a *Tyrannosaurus rex* in Michigan, there are places where you can hunt for the fossils of "Hexagonaria," a coral animal that lived in the warm seas during the same era. If that doesn't excite your kids, then tell them you are searching for a precious stone often hoarded by lapidaries (persons who practice the art of cutting and polishing gems) and sold in jewelry shops throughout the state.

Either way, it's easy and fun to collect Petoskey stones. It can be done along many shorelines in northern Michigan, but at Fisherman's Island State Park, it can be turned into a memorable camping trip where you might end up with a beachfront site, a place where your tent is only a few feet from the lapping waters of Lake Michigan.

The park is 5 miles south of Charlevoix and is reached from US-31 by turning west on Bell Bay Road, marked with a state park sign. Fisherman's Island maintains a ninety-site rustic campground, with the vast majority of sites located in a heavily wooded area. But ten to fifteen of them are right on the sandy shoreline of the Great Lake and are always the first chosen. If you're planning to spend more than one night, select an inland site and then transfer to a lakeshore spot whenever one opens up at 8:00 A.M.

From the check-in station, the park road follows the shoreline for 2.5 miles to the day-use area and swimming beach at the end, passing along the way many stretches of pebbled beaches. This is where you'll find rock hounds searching for Michigan's state stone. Petoskey stones are actually petrified coral, leftover fragments of the many reefs that existed in the warm-water seas from Charlevoix to Alpena 300 million years ago during the Paleozoic Era.

Dry Petoskey stones are silvery with no markings apparent to the untrained eye, but when the fossils are wet, it's easy to see the honeycomb pattern that covers them. Gem enthusiasts will walk slowly along the shore in about six inches of water, constantly picking up handfuls of pebbles and holding them just under the clear surface of the lake. Many stones will be only partially covered by the distinct pattern. The real find is locating the small round ones with the fossilized cells all over.

Store your gems in a glass jar filled with water and that way their patterns will always be on display. Searching for Petoskey stones is such a popular activity here that hand-outs are available at the check-in station explaining the natural history of the fossils.

■ 55.
NEBO
TRAIL
WILDERNESS STATE PARK

Activities: Skiing, frontier cabin
County: Emmet
Difficulty: Moderate to challenging
Length: 3 miles round-trip
Fee: Vehicle entry permit, cabin rental fee
Information: Park headquarters, (616) 436-5381

■ Camping in winter?

Sure, you say, and then entice them into this adventure with a description of an old-fashioned log cabin, surrounded by towering pine trees and hardwoods, and blanketed in a thick layer of snow.

The rustic interior of Nebo Cabin, Wilderness State Park

Imagine skiing through the woods and then spending a night in a snug cabin made pleasantly warm by a wood-burning stove. Spend the next day exploring the backcountry ski trails of Wilderness State Park and then ski out on the third day. Is there a better way to break up the monotony of a long Michigan winter?

The 7,514-acre park is located along the Straits of Mackinac and is reached from I-75 by departing west at exit 338 in Mackinaw City and following County Road 81. Signs mark the turn onto Wilderness Park Drive and 12 miles from the city you reach the park's entrance.

There are five "wilderness cabins" in the park, but Nebo is by far the best for a winter trip with children. The rest are located along the straits, where the winds off the lake can be strong and cold at times. Not only is Nebo surrounded by trees, but the trail to it is a 1.5-mile ski along a level route. Good snow for skiing can be anticipated from late December to mid-March; after that you're taking your chances. Regardless of when you go, book the cabin as far in advance as pos-

NEBO TRAIL

START

BIG STONE BAY

WILDERNESS

PARK

DRIVE

RED PINE TRAIL

MT. NEBO

HEMLOCK TRAIL

EAST RIDGE TRAIL

EAST BOUNDARY TRAIL

GOOSE POND

N

NEBO TRAIL

BIG

SUCKER CREEK

SWAMP LINE RD. TRAIL

E. BIG STONE CR.

NEBO CABIN

EAST BOUNDARY

TO STURGEON CABIN

STURGEON BAY TRAIL

SOUTH BOUNDARY TRAIL

WILDERNESS STATE PARK

0   ½   1 MILE

sible by writing to Wilderness State Park, Carp Lake, MI 49718.

During the winter the cabin is rented for a mandatory two nights on the weekends, but there is rarely a problem of driving to the park and skiing in by nightfall. The trailhead is located just before the organization camp on the south side of the park road or 1.5 miles east of the park headquarters. It's a wide trail where two persons can easily ski side-by-side and within 0.25 mile passes the first of two junctions to the Hemlock Trail.

The Hemlock Trail is a spur that climbs to the top of Mount Nebo. It's extremely steep and narrow in places and *should not be skied with young children.* The trail can be hiked (see 56. Mount Nebo and Big Stone Creek) and from fall to early spring there is a partial view through the trees of the straits. The Nebo Trail continues south and 0.5 mile from the second Hemlock junction passes the west end of the East

Ridge Trail and then crosses a small hill, the only rise on the trip.

It's not much farther until you ski around a corner and there is the cabin sitting on a small hill. Beautiful sight, but most parties don't stop to admire it; rather they rush in and begin a fire in the stove. Wood is provided by the park staff but remember to bring a small axe in case the last party didn't leave any kindling. It's amazing how quickly the stove will heat up the four-bunk structure.

SUMMER USE

You can also rent the unit during the summer, even driving to it if you wish. But the hike is so pleasant, it seems a shame not to walk in. To turn the trip into an overnight loop, continue south 0.5 mile to the junction with the South Boundary Trail. Head west on this trail for 1.4 miles and then north on Swamp Line Road Trail for 1.5 miles. This trail provides a dry route through the middle of an interesting cedar swamp. Pick up the wood-chip trail around Goose Pond to Red Pine Trail, which ends 1.2 miles to the east at Nebo Trail, 0.3 mile south of the trailhead.

56.
MOUNT NEBO
AND BIG STONE CREEK
WILDERNESS STATE PARK

Activities: Day hike, camping
County: Emmet
Difficulty: Moderate
Length: Loops of 3.9 to 4.6 miles
Fee: Vehicle entry fee, camping fee
Information: Park headquarters, (616) 436-5381

■ Four short trails can be linked together at Wilderness State Park to make for a delightful day hike though a variety of terrain and natural features. The trek includes following a

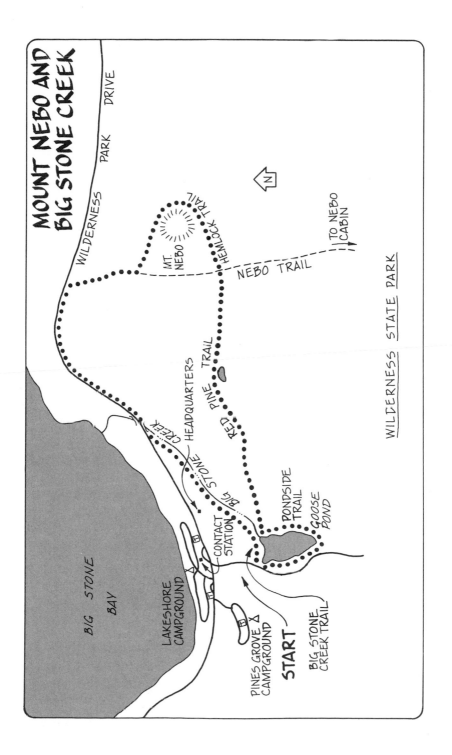

MOUNT NEBO AND
BIG STONE CREEK

WILDERNESS PARK DRIVE

N

MT. NEBO

HEMLOCK TRAIL

NEBO TRAIL

TO NEBO CABIN

WILDERNESS STATE PARK

RED PINE TRAIL

BIG STONE CREEK

HEADQUARTERS

CONTACT STATION

PONDSIDE TRAIL

GOOSE POND

BIG STONE BAY

LAKESHORE CAMPGROUND

PINES GROVE CAMPGROUND

START

BIG STONE CREEK TRAIL

Anglers fishing Goose Pond in Wilderness State Park

stream where there is considerable amount of beaver activity, climbing to the top of Mount Nebo for a glimpse of Lake Michigan, and skirting the edge of several ponds laden with wildlife.

Best of all, the main trailhead is located just a step away from the park's two campgrounds—one situated along the sandy shore of Big Stone Bay and the other in a grove of mature pines. Combine a night in the campground with the day hike in the morning and an afternoon spent on the bay's beautiful beaches, and you've put together an enjoyable outdoor adventure for children of any age.

The park's east entrance is 8 miles west of Mackinaw City and is reached by following County Road 81 and continuing west on Wilderness Park Drive after crossing Carp Lake River. Three of the four trails, Pondside, Red Pine, and Hemlock, have interpretive posts and the corresponding brochures can be obtained at the park headquarters or the contact station. You can shorten the loop to 3.9 miles by passing the Pondside Trail and beginning with the Red Pine Trail.

PONDSIDE TRAIL

The main trailhead is located just beyond the Pines Grove Campground entrance and is marked by a large display map. The Pondside Trail is a 0.7-mile loop around Goose Pond, with interpretive posts numbered in a clockwise direction. But many prefer hiking it in the opposite direction to avoid backtracking the top portion in order to continue on to the Red Pine. The trail never leaves the edge of the pond and features fifteen posts pointing out a variety of trees and other plants. At the south end, it crosses three wooden bridges, two of which extend over the top of beaver dams, allowing you to view the animal's handiwork: sticks on one side, mud on the other. This is also a common spot for children to fish for bluegill and other panfish.

RED PINE TRAIL

This 1.25-mile trail departs east at post number 7 of the Pondside Trail and immediately passes through a swamp area that at times can be a challenge in keeping your shoes dry. You climb out of the lowlands in 0.4 mile at post number 7 and follow a ridge to emerge at the trail's namesake halfway through the hike: a beautiful stand of red pine. You pass two ponds, descending to the second, larger one after first viewing it from above. Frogs will be croaking here and turtles scrambling off logs for the security of the water. If the bugs are not too bad, it's hard not to pause for a search of other critters. Beyond the second pond, the trail crosses one more swampy section to douse any shoes that have remained dry up to this point and then ascends to a junction on the Nebo Trail.

HEMLOCK TRAIL

Beginning just a short way up the Nebo Trail (see 55. Nebo Trail) is the 0.7-mile Hemlock Trail, a climb to the top of Mount Nebo. The first half is a steady but gradual march up the hill until you reach post number 24, the highpoint where the stone foundation of an old fire tower remains. Not much of a view during the summer, but in the spring and fall, you can see Lake Michigan to the north through the bare trees. The trail rapidly descends the peak and then passes some virgin hemlock pines at post number 26, huge trees that are more than 200 years old.

BIG STONE CREEK TRAIL

From the north end of the Hemlock Trail, it's a quarter mile along the Nebo Trail to Wilderness Park Drive and then 0.9 mile along the county road to the posted trailhead of the Big Stone Creek Trail across the parking lot from the park's day-use area. The trail is a level 0.7-mile walk that quickly comes to Big Stone Creek and then follows it to where man has dammed it to create Goose Pond. In the middle of the walk you'll see where beavers have dammed the creek themselves, causing it to flood the original trail. Today you can still see the side of the old trail in the middle of a pond. There are some great examples of gnawed trees surrounded by wood chips, and even a couple of beaver lodges, the best and largest 0.2 mile from the man-made dam. Eventually Big Stone Creek Trail merges into Pondside Trail and it's only a short walk west to the trailhead and display map.

Opposite: *Canoe adventure, Big Island Lake Wilderness*

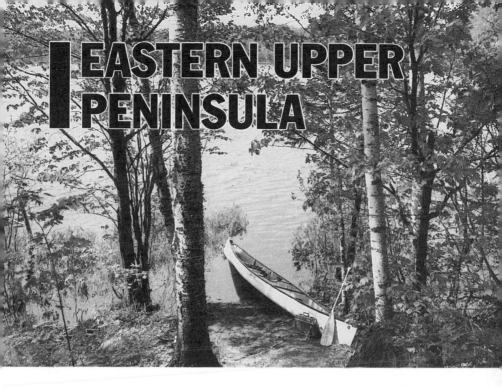

EASTERN UPPER PENINSULA

57.
BIG KNOB
AND CROW LAKE
LAKE SUPERIOR STATE FOREST

Activities: Day hike, camping
County: Mackinac
Difficulty: Easy to moderate
Length: Round-trips of 0.5 to 2.5 miles
Fee: Camping fee
Information: DNR Naubinway office, (906) 477-6262

■ A "Big Knob" to climb, an assortment of trails to hike, and one of the most beautiful beaches along Lake Michigan. What more could a kid want in a campground? As for the parents, the best part of Big Knob recreation area in Lake Superior State Forest is the lack of crowds.

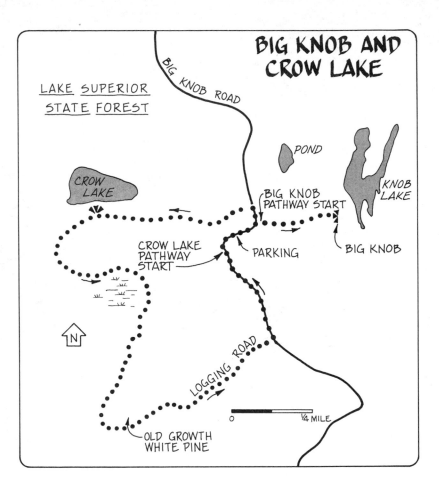

BIG KNOB AND CROW LAKE

LAKE SUPERIOR STATE FOREST

BIG KNOB ROAD

POND

CROW LAKE

KNOB LAKE

BIG KNOB PATHWAY START

CROW LAKE PATHWAY START

PARKING

BIG KNOB

N

LOGGING ROAD

0   ¼ MILE

OLD GROWTH WHITE PINE

Maybe the facility will fill up during the Fourth of July weekend, but the rest of the summer you can usually count on getting a site in the rustic campground. Arrive during the middle of the week or at the end of August to obtain a site just inside the towering pines along the Lake Michigan shoreline, where your tent will be only a few steps from the golden sand and light blue waters of the Great Lake.

The area is reached after driving the scenic lakeside portion of US-2, beginning with a trip over the Mackinac Bridge. From I-75, head west on the highway for 50 miles, passing through Naubinway and then turning south (left) on Big

View from the top of Big Knob, Lake Superior State Forest

Knob Road. It's 6 miles along the narrow and winding road to the campground on Lake Michigan, and along the way you'll pass the trailheads for two of the three treks in the area. The third, Marsh Lakes Pathway (not discussed here), is a 1.5-mile, one-way trail that begins from the parking area of the campground's picnic area.

BIG KNOB PATHWAY

The shortest trail is the 0.25-mile climb to Big Knob, a high point on a forested sand dune. The posted trailhead is 3.5 miles south along Big Knob Road, right across the parking area from Crow Lake Pathway. The trail is basically a steady, but not overly exerting, climb to the viewing point, where there is a bench and a U.S. Geological Survey marker.

Along the way are three sets of log stairways and a view of a small pond to the north. The trail ends at the top of Big Knob and here you are greeted with a panorama of Knob Lake below and the marshland that surrounds it. It's an excellent view, especially in spring and early fall when large flocks of Canada geese often use the lake as a staging area. You see them and hear them, and often the honking greets you before you even begin the hike.

CROW LAKE PATHWAY

The pathway has three trailheads, including the first right across from Big Knob. It's a 2.5-mile loop to walk the trail and return along Big Knob Road to your vehicle. From the first trailhead, you begin with a steady climb to the top of a sand dune ridge and then follow the gently rolling contour of its crest. Within 0.3 mile you come to the posted junction with the second trailhead and then at 0.7 mile a good view of Crow Lake.

After passing above the lake, the trail gently descends off the ridge and passes through open areas that feature an impressive growth of ferns. But if it's August, examine the ground along the trail (or have the children do it—they're closer to it anyhow). This is blueberry country, and if the timing is right there will be dots of blue all over the place. At 1.3 miles, the trail passes the largest of several marsh areas, one with an interpretive display explaining its importance to wildlife.

You climb up and over a low dune ridge and then emerge at a rather interesting area. To the right is a clear cut, to the left a preserved stand of old white pine, some so large two people couldn't connect their hands around them. All of this demonstrates the multiple-use concept of state forest management, which may mean little to most children. What will have a profound effect on them is the sign that reads "Lightning Damaged Pine." Behind it are a pair of white pines that are broken in half, the tops of their massive trunks shattered into a dozen pieces.

You reach an old logging road at 1.8 miles with a few more interpretive signs that make this an educational as well as a scenic hike, and at 2.1 miles you return to Big Knob Road. It's a 0.4 mile walk up the road to the first trailhead.

58.
MARSHLAND
WILDLIFE DRIVE
SENEY NATIONAL WILDLIFE REFUGE

Activities: Scenic drive, interpretive center, birding
County: Schoolcraft
Difficulty: Easy
Length: 7-mile loop
Fee: None
Information: Refuge headquarters, (906) 586-9851

■ The first thing you notice at the Seney National Wildlife Refuge visitor's center are all the Canada geese walking around. At 95,455 acres, Seney is one of two national wildlife refuges in Michigan and the largest one east of the Mississippi River.

Seney is reached from M-77 by turning west onto a posted refuge road 2 miles north of Germfask or 5 miles south from the town of Seney. Follow the refuge road to the visitor's center, where you will be greeted by dozens of tame geese mingling around the cars and building, looking for a possible handout.

The second thing you will notice about the refuge are all the droppings on the parking lot. The black top is literally splatted with white. Take it in stride (or tip-toe through it), for it's all part of experiencing a wildlife sanctuary, where you'll have excellent opportunities for viewing birds, mammals, deer, and even an eagle's nest through the window of your car.

Begin with the impressive visitor's center, built on a large

---

pond with one side a huge glass wall set up with telescopes so visitors can view the birdlife on the surrounding marshes. There are also displays on the history, ecology, and wildlife of the refuge, hands-on exhibits for children, and an auditorium that shows nature films every hour. The interpretive center is open 9:00 A.M. to 5:00 P.M. daily from mid-May to the end of September.

After taking in the exhibits, grab a "Marshland Wildlife Drive" booklet, pack the children in the car, and follow the 7-mile, self-guided auto tour. The drive begins near the visitor center and ends on M-77 just south of the refuge entrance. It takes about an hour to follow the single-lane dirt track around four ponds, while stopping at twenty posted stations keyed to the information in the booklet.

Unlike the Canada geese around the visitor center, the wildlife seen along this drive are truly wild and can be viewed in their own environment. The tour points out a variety of habitats—wetlands, open water, and forest communities. You'll see nesting islands used by geese, nesting boxes that are used by wood ducks and hooded mergansers, and sandy banks where kingfishers have excavated homes into the soft soil. It's possible at times to spot loons, herons, muskrats, and beavers swimming through the water, or deer on the edge of the forests. But the high point for many is station 12, where you view an active eagle's nest that measures 8 feet across and 5 feet deep near the top of a dying red pine.

There is also a 1.4-mile nature trail beginning and ending from the visitor center for those who want to get out for a walk. But the auto tour is the best way to see and learn about wildlife. The drive is open during daylight hours from June 1 to October 15. Bring a high-power scope or binoculars for a better view of the animals and keep in mind that spring, late summer, and fall are the best seasons for wildlife viewing and that animals are most active in morning and evening hours. Throughout the summer, evening tours are led by staff naturalists and the dates and times can be obtained by calling the refuge.

59.
AU SABLE
LIGHT STATION
PICTURED ROCKS NATIONAL LAKESHORE

Activities: Day hike, camping
County: Alger
Difficulty: Easy
Length: 3 miles round-trip
Fee: Camping fee
Information: Grand Marais Ranger Station, (906) 494-2669

Pictured Rocks National Lakeshore is a nice place to visit during the summer and spectacular during the fall colors of late September. But many feel the best time to undertake this adventure is in November, when the skies are gray and Lake Superior is crashing along the rocky shoreline. The camping might be a little chilly and it could even snow then, but there's not a better backdrop for enjoying the unusual maritime flavor of this trail.

The easy and level walk combines the rugged shoreline of the Great Lake with scattered remains of shipwrecks and the preserved Au Sable Light Station. One, of course, is directly responsible for the other. The stretch from Au Sable

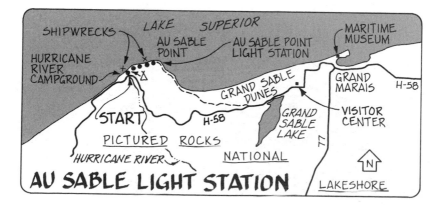

Point, where the lighthouse is perched, to Whitefish Point to the east was known as "the graveyard of the Great Lakes" to sailors in the 1800s, as dozens of ships perished along the exposed shoreline. The Au Sable Light Station was built in 1874 and manned until the U.S. Coast Guard automated it in 1958. Today there is still a light at the top of the tower to warn ships of the shoals off Au Sable Point, while the rest of the station is now listed on the National Register of Historic Places and under the care of the National Park Service.

Just getting to the trail is an adventure. Begin in Grand Marais with a stop at the Maritime Museum and ranger station. Open from 10:00 A.M. to 5:30 P.M. daily from May through mid-September, the museum features the lighthouse Frensel lens, as well as uniforms, a Lyle gun, and other equipment used by the lifesaving crew that lived there. From the small and picturesque town, head west on County Road H-58, past Grand Sable Lake and the sand dunes trying to creep across the road. From here the road plunges into a thick forest as it curves and winds its way toward Munising, a 50-mile trip. Your stop is Hurricane River Campground, 12 miles from Grand Marais.

Head to the lower level of the campground, a pleasant area to pitch a tent, where every site is a short walk from the sandy beach. The shoreline makes for a nice stroll, but Lake Superior is usually too cold for even the bravest (most foolhardy?) souls to swim in. A bridge crosses Hurricane River and allows the Lakeshore Trail to continue through the campground and merge into a lighthouse access road on the east side. A gate marks the beginning of the old access road, but a "Shipwreck" sign next to it has you scrambling down to the beach. These ruins lie about 20 yards off the beach and are hard to see clearly when there is a chop on the water.

Tell the children not to be disappointed. Better ones lie ahead.

The old track skirts the shoreline from above and soon you see the sandy beach give way to a rocky coast. Some stretches are strewn with small boulders while others are solid slaps of red rock whose surface has been sculptured into a se-

Au Sable Light Station, Pictured Rocks National Lakeshore

ries of ripples by centuries of waves washing ashore. At almost a mile from the gate you arrive at the second shipwreck sign. After descending to the beach, it's 1,500 feet to the east (right) to the first remains. These lie on the beach, and the timbers and ironwork joining them make it appear as if they were the hull of a ship. Two more sets of ruins lie farther up the beach. The best way to return to the trail for families with small children is to backtrack to the sign, instead of scaling the tall, sandy bluffs.

The light station is only a short walk from the shipwrecks and features a number of buildings: the keeper's residence, boat house, fog signal house, even a red brick privy. But the most impressive structure by far is the lighthouse, with its tower projecting light 107 feet above Lake Superior. Interpretive displays throughout the station explain the history and functions behind each building. The lighthouse itself was renovated as a 1910 keeper's residence and will be open to the public in 1991. The best part of the entire walk is the climb to the top of the tower. It's 100 steps up but the view of the Grand Sable Dunes is unsurpassed anywhere in the park.

60. PICTURED ROCKS
PICTURED ROCKS NATIONAL LAKESHORE

Activity: Scenic cruise
County: Alger
Difficulty: Easy
Length: 2.5- to 3-hour trip
Fee: Tour boat fee
Information: Picture Rocks Cruises, Inc., (906) 387-2379

■ It seems like anytime children board a boat, it's an adventure, but this is one of the best boats to venture on in Michigan. The 3-hour trip skirts along the famous Pictured Rocks, where most kids are fascinated by the sheer cliffs, stunning

Miner's Castle, the most famous formation of the Pictured Rocks

colors of the rocks, and the unusual formations that look like Indians, battleships, or castles. Occasionally Lake Superior is too rough for young stomachs and kids under the age of five might get restless before the trip is over, though that can be cured by bringing a lunch and enough snacks along.

You can drive to the most famous formation, Miner's Castle, with trails skirting the high bluffs along the shoreline, but the only way to see the amazing bands of colors or to appreciate the overwhelming size of the cliffs is to view them from the water. Besides, boat rides are fun and if the sun is shining and the lake smooth, this cruise is often the highlight of many vacations in the Upper Peninsula, regardless of age.

Picture Rock Cruises, Incorporated operates all three of its boats from a large dock in downtown Munising, a scenic city surrounded by green hills on three sides and protective

Munising Bay on the other. Cruises are scheduled daily from June through mid-October. During the peak of the summer season, July and August, there are five cruises every day, from 9:00 A.M. until 5:00 P.M. From mid-June until June 30 and during September, two trips are offered each day, one at 10:00 A.M. and the other at 2:00 P.M. From June 1 until mid-June and from the end of September through the fall colors, there is one trip a day at 1:00 P.M.

The adventure begins by scrambling onto the large vessels and then sailing out of Munising Bay, past the old Grand Island Lighthouse into the freshwater sea that is Lake Superior. It isn't long before the first rock formation, Miner's Castle, comes into view. While children try to envision it being a castle, the captain of the tour boat explains how legend has it that in 1688 Father Jacques Marquette, the famous Jesuit explorer, delivered a sermon from the edge of the rock to a tribe of Chippewa Indians bobbing in canoes below.

The sandstone cliffs, that at times reach heights of 200 feet above the lake, intensify in color because of the seepage of underlying minerals. The bands of browns, golds, and reds change each hour with the rising or setting sun, but there is little question how this strip of shoreline picked up its name. Wind and constant wave action of a stormy Lake Superior has carved caves, arches, and other formations out of the cliffs. Especially impressive is the Colored Caves. The Indians referred to them as Caves of Bloody Chiefs because they were sure their enemies had left war prisoners there to be dashed to pieces. The formation is that red.

Such Indian tales thrill children who spend much of the trip hanging onto the railing of the ship. But the impressive moment comes after you pass the formation known as Indian Head and a gull rookery. Between the rookery and Battleship Rock, the tour ship pauses at a formation known as Portal. If the water is calm, the captain maneuvers the ship inside this cove, where cliffs of sandstone tower above you with their distinctive bands of color.

So overwhelming is this unusual perspective of Pictured Rocks that even children as young as four or five realize this is a very special part of Michigan that should be cherished and treasured.

61.
KITCHI-ITI-KIPI
SPRING
PALMS BOOK STATE PARK

Activities: Scenic view, raft ride
County: Schoolcraft
Difficulty: Easy
Fee: Vehicle entry permit
Information: Indian Lake State Park, (906) 341-2355

■ The state's largest natural spring is the destination for an excellent family adventure, especially for children too young to endure a long day hike. Located in Palms Book State Park, Kitchi-Iti-Kipi is one of Michigan's most intriguing natural wonders, combining the fantasy world of the spring with an adventurous raft trip for viewing it. The only walking involved is a 5-minute stroll from the parking lot to the dock and raft.

Palms Book State Park is 8 miles north on M-149 from US-2, making it a quick side trip and welcome break for families traveling across the Upper Peninsula. There is no campground at the state park, but a shaded picnic area is near the springs, along with restrooms and a concession store.

Pick up a handout at the contact station of the park, read the Indian tales and history that surround the spring, and then head to a small dock at the west end of the pond. Here visitors board a 15-by-15-foot wooden raft that features a viewing area in the middle. A steel cable strung across the spring is used by the strongest member of any party to pull the raft across, while everybody else enjoys the view below the surface.

Kitchi-Iti-Kipi is a Chippewa word that has been assigned many meanings, but perhaps the best description for this area (also called "Big Spring") is "Mirror of Heaven." The natural spring is 200 feet long and 40 feet deep, and more than 10,000 gallons of crystal-clear water pour out every minute from narrow openings in the underlying limestone. The temperature of the water never changes, it's always forty-five degrees summer or winter, but the "heavenly" underwater view does.

Between the swirls of sand and ghostly bubbles rising up, you can view sunken trees with branches encrusted in limestone, huge brown trout slipping silently by, and colors and shapes that come and go. It's a fantasy world that sparks the imagination of children and made one visitor remark, "You have to come back to make sure you saw what you think you did."

The picnic area makes the park a good lunch time destination, but early morning is especially enchanting, as often a mist lies over the water while the trout are rising to the surface. During the winter the entrance gate is locked after the first snowfall, but visitors park outside and hike in for a raft trip across this alluring attraction.

62.
NINGA AKI
PATHWAY
LAKE SUPERIOR STATE FOREST

Activities: Day hike, camping
County: Delta
Difficulty: Easy
Length: Loops of 1.5 to 2.2 miles
Fee: Camping fee
Information: DNR Thompson office, (906) 341-6971

■ One of Michigan's most secluded shoreline campgrounds accessible by car is located on the east side of the Upper Peninsula's Garden Peninsula, with twenty-four sites on the edge of Portage Bay. All the sites are well hidden among the towering red pines that border the bay, but three steps from your tent is the sandy beach and clear waters of Lake Michigan.

This adventure begins before you even reach the campground. From the town of Garden in the middle of the peninsula, head south on County Road 483 for 2 miles to the junction known as Devil's Corner. Curve to the west and you'll head for Fayette State Park, where an abandoned 1880 mining town has been renovated and today is called Michigan's "most popular ghost town."

But continue straight on the gravel road posted "state forest campground" to reach Portage Bay. Turn left on Lane 12.75 and then hang on. The rugged dirt road bumps and grinds for 5 miles on its way to the east shore. Occasionally you'll pass the driveway to a remote cottage, but most of the time the road is the only opening in the thick pine forest. Just before you accept your children's greatest fear—we're lost forever—the campground sign appears.

Pink lady slippers along Ninga Aki Pathway at Portage Bay Campground

This is a rustic campground with vault toilets, hand pump for water, and fire rings and picnic tables at every site. The rustic facilities only enhance the experience of spending a night at remote Portage Bay—a crescent-moon beach, lined by pines and enclosed by a pair of rocky points at each end. Nearby is Ninga Aki Pathway, a 2.2-mile network of trails. The 1.5-mile Lake Michigan Loop is marked by a display sign at the north end of the campground and begins next to site number 1. Ninga Aki is an Objiway word that means "Mother Earth," and posts along the trail point out the staples of Indians life here when they lived off the land. Though many of the posts are missing, trail guides can be obtained ahead of time by writing to Information Services, DNR, Box 30028, Lansing, MI 48909.

The trail comes to a junction, where you head west (left) to follow the numbered interpretive posts. Post number 1 points out juniper berries, which Indians used to boil into a thick, soft mush. You pass the junction to the Bog Loop and then use a long row of planking to cross a wet area through a stand of hemlock. Post number 5 points out a white spruce. Indians would soak the roots of these trees and lace birch bark canoes together with them. Post number 6, reached at 0.5 mile from the beginning, is a balsam fir; balsam resin waterproofed the seams of Objiway boats. At this point the trail is heading east toward the water and you can hear the waves as you approach post number 9, identifying an example of white pine, whose seeds the Objiway used to flavor venison and bear meat.

The trail reaches Portage Bay at its rocky northern end. It's hard to distinguish the trail at times, but for the next 0.4 mile you follow the bay's edge between the trees and the open shoreline. You'll pick up stretches of the trail here and there, always with a scenic view of the bay. At 1.3 miles from the trailhead, the loop finishes as a well-defined path leading back into the woods to the junction. You can end the walk here or, if young legs are willing, extend it another mile to the Bog Loop junction and then head south along the spur.

The trail, 0.75 mile long, quickly crosses the end of the first bog, which contains very little open water. The hiking can get wet in some places before you come to the second pond in 0.3 mile, labeled on some maps as Charboneau Lake. Surrounding the small, scenic lakes are ideal conditions for locating pink lady's slipper, one of the state's most beautiful orchids. The trail continues past the lake for almost another 0.5 mile before it swings sharply east and emerges at the road at an unmarked location.

▌63.
KLONDIKE
LAKE
BIG ISLAND LAKE WILDERNESS

Activities: Canoeing, fishing
County: Schoolcraft
Difficulty: Moderate
Length: 3- to 4-day paddle
Fee: None
Information: Munising Ranger District, (906) 387-2512

■ One of nine federally designated wilderness areas created in 1987, Big Island Lake Wilderness consists of twenty-three small lakes, ranging from 5 to 149 acres and situated among low rolling hills of hardwood forests and stands of spruce and hemlock. The lakes are small enough to be easily paddled, even with a child in the bow, the portages are short enough so you don't suffer too much carrying the canoe, and the entire area is remote enough to give you a sense of being in a wilderness.

An ideal trip is to begin at Big Island Lake, camping along the shoreline or at one of its islands the first night. The next day paddle Mid Lake, Coattail, and McInnes lakes, making four portages to spend the night at Klondike Lake in the heart of the wilderness. Unfortunately, there is no way to do a complete loop among the lakes, so backtracking is in order. This is fine for most people, however, because the scenery is good, the wildlife plentiful, and the fishing usually very productive. In all, this makes for an excellent canoeing adventure for children six to eight who have already spent some time in the boat.

Big Island Lake is reached from Munising by heading east on M-28 for 3 miles and then south on H-13 for 9 miles. Turn east (left) onto County Road 445, which is posted by a small white sign and follow it 3.5 miles to a small parking area with a Forest Service bulletin board off to one side. Across the road is the portage (large boulders block vehicles from entering it), and the walk is only 0.2 mile to the lake.

Big Island Lake is the largest of all and is marked in the middle by a pair of islands. It's a quick 15-minute paddle to the west side of the largest one, traditionally a popular camping area. Another excellent place to camp is near the Mid Lake portage, east of the small island and marked by an orange and yellow sign of a canoeist. Here you can camp on top of a low ridge and have a view of both lakes from the door of your tent. Fishing is good in the large lake for smallmouth bass, northern pike, panfish, and muskies, though special fishing regulations (no live bait) are in effect. Check the current Michigan Department of Natural Resources fishing guide for all the regulations.

The portage to Mid Lake is a carry of only 100 feet and puts you near the west end of the narrow lake. Mid Lake was stocked for brook trout in recent years, but anglers who toss small spinners among the deadheads along the shore often end up catching largemouth bass. The portage to Coattail is located at the east end and is well marked and visible. The trail is only 400 feet long but does climb a ridge—the reason, no doubt, for the canoe rest at the top.

Coattail is the widest lake you'll pass through and can be fished for northern pike and perch, which young anglers have an easier time landing. Or just paddle it slowly with an eye out for wildlife. Loons and other waterfowl, great blue heron, and even an occasional eagle can be spotted. White-tailed deer and black bear reside in the Big Island Lake Wilderness, and, to see the work of a beaver, paddle beyond the marked portage at the east end to the huge dam that has reduced a stream to a trickle of water.

The portage to McInnes Lake is 0.25 mile long, climbs another ridge, and passes another canoe rest before descend-

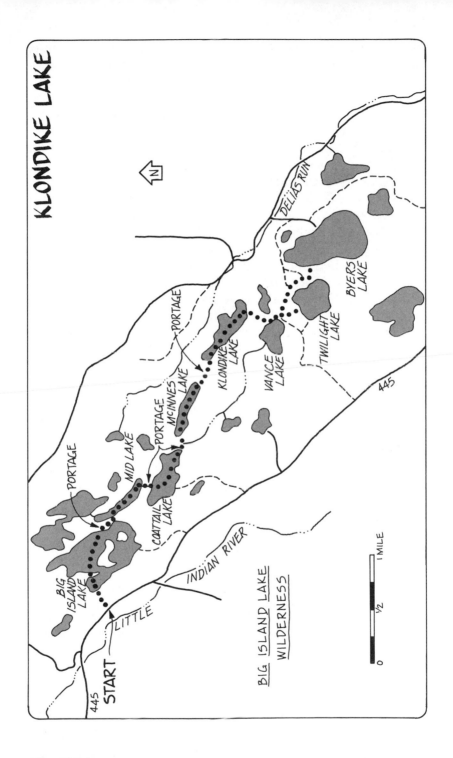

KLONDIKE LAKE

N

DELIAS RUN

BYERS LAKE

TWILIGHT LAKE

KLONDIKE LAKE

VANCE LAKE

445

PORTAGE

MCINNES LAKE

PORTAGE

MID LAKE

PORTAGE

COATTAIL LAKE

INDIAN RIVER

BIG ISLAND LAKE WILDERNESS

BIG ISLAND LAKE

LITTLE

START

445

0   ½   1 MILE

ing to the next lakeshore. McInnes has a weedy shoreline, making it tough to find a good campsite. The final portage is located at the southeast corner of McInnes and is posted and visible. The 0.3-mile portage is a level walk before it climbs a low ridge and then drops to the bog area surrounding the west end of Klondike. No planking here, but logs have been laid out to help you cross the wet area to the open water. It's a bit of a "wilderness challenge," especially if you're balancing a canoe on your shoulders.

Klondike is worth it, however. It's a beautiful lake, with many coves and small peninsulas, and hemmed in by paper birch whose white bark is reflected in the water on still evenings. A lot of good places to camp, but some of the best are at the tip of the points along the north shore. The fishing is excellent for northern pike or you can spend some time hiking around Vance and Twilight lakes, beginning at the posted portage trail at the east end.

To return you simply retrace the route. The portage at the west end of Klondike is hard to spot from the water because of the weedy shoreline. Look for the portage marker on a birch stump and search for the opening in the weeds.

64.
TYOGA
TOWNSITE
ESCANABA STATE FOREST

Activities: Day hike, camping
County: Alger
Difficulty: Easy
Length: 1.4-mile loop
Fee: Campsite fee
Information: DNR Marquette office, (906) 228-6561

A lost logging town was rediscovered when the personal accounts of two Upper Peninsula men were recently pieced together with newspaper articles, county historical records, and labor records, allowing Tyoga to emerge from a faded past. Based on the information and photos that were found, the Tyoga Historical Pathway was built in 1988 and today provides hikers not only a pleasant forest walk but an interesting glimpse into a turn-of-the-century lumber town.

The 1.4-mile loop is an easy hike but wet at times, and boots are recommended most of the summer. Along the way there are twenty-two interpretive posts, each providing in words or photos a view of life in old Tyoga. The logging pathway is located 23 miles west of Munising, via M-28. Turn north at the Deerton turnoff and follow the dirt road for 2 miles to the Laughing Whitefish State Forest Campground, where the trailhead is well marked. Plan on 45 minutes to an hour to walk the trail and read all the interpretive signs. Stay for lunch or even pitch a tent to stay overnight at the beautiful campground which borders the Laughing Whitefish River.

In 1902 a group of Pennsylvania businessmen, spurred on by the nation's growing demand for white pine, purchased the eventual townsite of Tyoga and 1,200 adjacent acres. When the Tyoga Lumber Company was incorporated in 1905, three million board feet of logs had already been cut from the woods surrounding the thriving lumbering town. The trail begins on the banks of Laughing Fish River (as it was known then) and the first few posts discuss the millpond that was formed and the two-story mill powered by an Atlas steam engine. You can still see the foundations that held the 130-horsepower engine whose ban saw cut 50,000 board feet of pine and hemlock in ten hours.

From here the trail crosses a bridge over the river, follows the opposite banks briefly, and then swings into the woods. Along the way you read about "Game Warden Eddy" and Irishman Dan McEachern, whose logging crew included thirty-two lumberjacks and four women cooks. At 0.7 mile, the trail crosses a stream and enters what's left of the clearing that surrounded Tyoga, a town that included not only the mill but a company store, a cook shanty capable of seating up to forty men at once, a boarding house, and ten private homes where lumberjacks paid twenty-five cents a day to stay, laundry service included.

The railroad grade is at post number 12 and at one time

you could board a Duluth-South Shore and Atlantic train here for a trip to Detroit. Price of a one-way ticket back then—six dollars and fifty cents. You cross another gurgling stream, learn that the white pine was 5 feet in diameter and 150 feet tall when the loggers cut the trees, and at post number 16 read about the children of Tyoga. During the summers, the youngsters fished for brook trout that often weighed up to three and a half pounds. They knew the best time to catch the trout was when the dam was open to let the water out for a log drive. Then they would take a wheelbarrow and, according to the interpretive sign, "pick up the trout that were left high and dry."

You recross the Laughing Fish River at 1.2 miles and pass five more interpretive signs, covering everything from popular hunting weapons of the day to a pack of timber wolves that once roamed the area, before returning to the campground. Through words and pictures along the trail, this pathway helps children gain insights into an important era in Michigan's past, without making it seem like a history lesson.

Opposite: *The Union Impoundment, stocked with brook trout each spring, Porcupine Mountains Wilderness State Park*

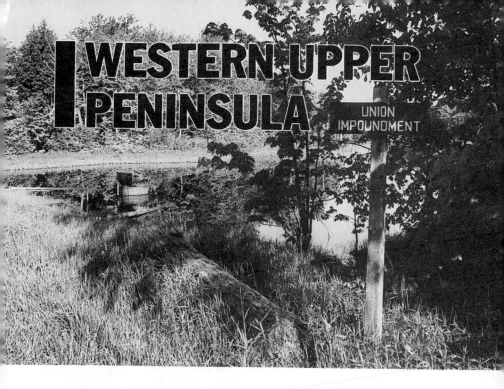

65.
PIERS
GORGE

PIERS GORGE SCENIC AREA

Activities: Day hike, rafting
County: Dickinson
Difficulty: Easy to moderate
Length: 3 miles round-trip
Fee: None
Information: Upper Peninsula Travel and Recreation Association in Iron Mountain, (906) 774-5480

Michigan's wildest white water is the stretch of the Menominee River that flows through Piers Gorge, 2 miles south of Norway on the state border with Wisconsin. Here the river has sliced through bedrock to form an area of holes, hydrau-

The whitewater at Piers Gorge attracts kayakers and rafters from around the Midwest.

lics, swirls, and a 10-foot drop known to rafters and kayakers as "Misicot." The hike offers an impressive display of white-water rafting, especially if you arrive on Saturday or Sunday afternoon when local rafting companies are running trips through the gorge.

To sit on the edge of the gorge and watch rubber rafts crash into swirls of white water is exciting for children and adults alike. To be in that raft going over a 10-foot drop . . . well, that's another whole adventure.

The area is owned by Consumers Power and is reached by heading south of Norway on US-8. Just before crossing the bridge to the Wisconsin side of the Menominee River, a sign for the Piers Gorge Scenic Area directs you to turn west (right). The paved road quickly becomes dirt, at which point you veer left. In 0.5 mile it ends at a parking area and a wide path continues west into the woods.

In 0.2 mile you hear the roar of the river and see the first of dozens of spurs that depart for the side of the gorge. The drop known as Misicot is reached in 0.5 mile, where you stand on the rocky edge of the canyon and watch water crash through a vicious stretch of holes, falls, and whirlpools. It's an impressive sight and the roar of white water is so loud your child will have to yell in your ear through cupped hands just to say, "I have to go to the bathroom."

The trail stays in sight of the white water for a little longer and then at 0.8 mile swings away from the river to become a shady and quiet walk in the forest. At 1 mile you emerge at the power-line right-of-way and then reenter the forest on the other side to come to a V junction in 0.3 mile. Blue diamonds mark the right fork, but head down the left-hand one to see the first falls and the start of the white water.

The falls is a one-way hike of 1.5 miles and makes for a good spot to turn around or enjoy lunch. To the west the river is calm, to the east it's entering its first rock chute. Between the two, a small rock spit sticks out into the river, where more than one young hiker has soaked tired feet before heading back. For those wanting to experience the rapids, not just view them, there is a Wisconsin rafting company that runs this stretch throughout the summer. Contact Argosy Adventures at (715) 251-3886.

▌66.
▌SUGARLOAF
▌MOUNTAIN
SUGARLOAF RECREATION TRAIL

Activity: Day hike
County: Marquette
Difficulty: Easy
Length: 1.2 miles round-trip
Fee: None
Information: Marquette Area Chamber of Commerce, (906) 226-6591

■ There are not many mountains to scale around Michigan, but an ideal "peak" for a child's first summit is located north of the city of Marquette in the Upper Peninsula. A hike up the Sugarloaf Recreation Trail combines a pleasant walk along a wooded path, a little climbing, and a peak at the end with a glorious 360-degree view of the surrounding country-side and Lake Superior. Although there are numerous stairs to climb, this short trail can be managed even by three- and four-year-olds when plenty of rest stops are taken.

The trail, maintained by the Marquette County Road Commission, is located 5 miles north of the city. Head out of Marquette on County Road 550, the road to Big Bay, and look for a dirt parking lot and a large Sugarloaf sign on the east side. This is an excellent lunchtime trail, so pack along some sandwiches and enjoy a picnic while viewing the Lake Superior shoreline. Bring something to drink, though, because there is no water along the way.

On the edge of the parking lot is an information sign and from there the trail beings as a wide path through the forest. Quickly it begins to climb, but benches here and there allow young legs to rest, while long staircases aid hikers over ridges and outcroppings of granite and gneiss. In 0.6 mile you climb 315 feet before breaking out of the trees to the rocky knob at top, marked by a stone monument.

The top of the 1,075-foot-high peak provides one of the best vistas of the area, affording fine views in every direction. Most people, however, concentrate on the panorama to the east, where you gaze upon the shoreline, the islands offshore, the city of Marquette, and the horizon of Lake Superior. For most, the trip back is a fast scramble down the trail to the parking lot.

67. CRAIG LAKE

CRAIG LAKE STATE PARK

Activities: Cabin rental, backpacking, canoeing
County: Baraga
Difficulty: Easy to challenging
Length: 1.5-mile hike to cabins
Fee: Vehicle entry permit, cabin fee
Information: Van Riper State Park, (906) 339-4461

Craig Lake State Park can be either a child's first trip into a wilderness area or an overnight backpacking adventure in a rugged corner of Michigan. The 6,983-acre park is a state-designated wilderness that at one time was the "getaway retreat" of a national brewery executive, who built a pair of cabins on the shore of Craig Lake. The Department of Natural Resources acquired the land and today rents out the cabins. The facilities feature beds, wood-burning stoves, limited utensils, and a LP gas refrigerator and lights.

The cabins offer a comfortable place to spend a night in the middle of a woods. The only way to reach the facilities is

Canoeists paddling to a campsite, Craig Lake, Craig Lake State Park

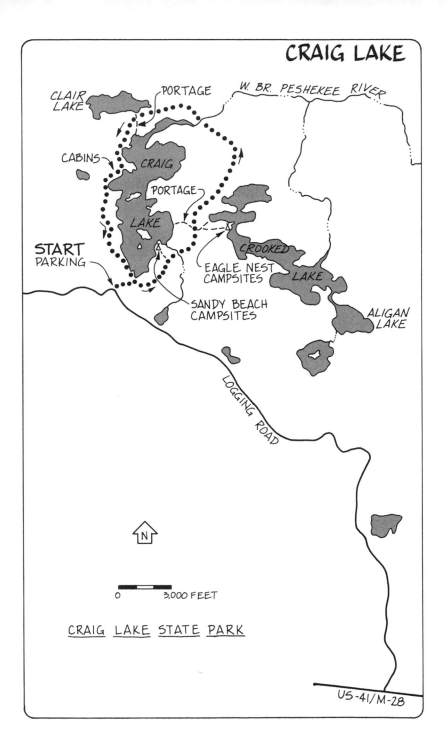

CRAIG LAKE

CLAIR LAKE

PORTAGE

W. BR. PESHEKEE RIVER

CABINS

CRAIG

PORTAGE

LAKE

START
PARKING

EAGLE NEST
CAMPSITES

CROOKED

LAKE

ALIGAN
LAKE

SANDY BEACH
CAMPSITES

LOGGING ROAD

N

0 — 3,000 FEET

CRAIG LAKE STATE PARK

US-41/M-28

either a 1.5-mile hike or a portage and a 30- to 45-minute paddle across the lake. Both are easy excursions, especially the hike, and can be handled by most children, even those as young as four or five. The cabins are popular, especially with anglers, and must be reserved in advance by calling or writing to Manager, Van Riper State Park, P.O. Box 66, Champion, MI 49814.

The most difficult aspect of the adventure is reaching the parking area, the only other facility in the park. The posted entrance to Craig Lake is Keewaydin Lake Road, a dirt vehicle track situated 7.9 miles west of Van Riper State Park on US-41/M-28. From here it is a 6.6-mile trip to the parking area along logging roads that can be very badly rutted or washed out. Additional roads and a lack of signs can make the trip very confusing without a detailed map. All parties entering the park should first stop at Van Riper State Park headquarters and pick up a Craig Lake Access map that contains the exact mileage from one turn to the next.

At the parking area, a yellow gate crosses the portage trail to Craig Lake, a 0.2-mile level walk to the lakeshore. A camping area is maintained here, while a foot trail, resembling a logging road, continues almost due north around the west side of the lake. Within 0.7 mile you cross a bridge over an unnamed river and then resume heading north. The trail becomes a more gently rolling path, passes a scenic view of the lake from a high bank, and then arrives at the cabins in 1.3 miles.

The logging road stops at the large cabin and beyond that the trail resembles a path in the forest. It is extremely scenic but does require considerably more climbing. A good afternoon hike for children six to eight is the walk to a high point on a rocky bluff, reached 1.1 miles up the trail.

The entire loop around Craig Lake is a 6.5-mile trek and makes for an excellent overnight trip. From the parking area, head east along the opposite shore of the cabins to reach Sandy Beach Campsite in 1 mile. The sites feature fire rings, tent pads, and a vault toilet on a high bluff overlooking the lake's largest island. Or you can continue north another 0.8 mile and then head east on a posted spur to the Eagle Nest Campsites, which overlook Crooked Lake. The following day would be used to complete the rest of the loop and would include some long climbs and descents of ridges and bluffs, but also a variety of viewing points. Most children should be eight to ten before tackling this route in two days.

With a canoe, visitors can portage into Clair Lake, north of Craig Lake, a popular lake with bass anglers, or take an overnight trip into Crooked Lake. The 0.5-mile portage is posted on the southeast side of Craig Lake and leads past Eagle Nest Campsite to a narrow inlet on Crooked Lake. It's possible to paddle the 270-acre and well-named Crooked Lake to a bay in its southeast corner where there is a quarter-mile passage into Aligan Lake. A second stream flows between Aligan's west shore and an unnamed lake to the south, which features a 3.5-acre island in the middle.

68.
CANYON FALLS
AND GORGE
CANYON FALLS ROADSIDE AREA

Activity: Day hike
County: Baraga
Difficulty: Easy
Length: 1 to 2 miles round-trip
Fee: None
Information: Baraga County Tourist Association, (906) 524-7444

■ Not all rest areas consist of picnic tables, trash cans, and a pair of vault toilets. A Michigan Department of Transportation roadside park on US-41 also serves as the trailhead to a beautiful falls and a stunning rock canyon, the largest box canyon in the state. On that long drive across the Upper Peninsula, Canyon Falls Roadside Area lets children and their parents stretch their legs by undertaking an easy, 1- to 2-mile hike before continuing on.

The roadside park is on the west side of US-41, 8 miles south of L'anse or 60 miles west of Marquette. The Department of Transportation maintains the rest area, but it was forestry students from Michigan Technological University who built the path and constructed the wooden boardwalks and observation platforms that make this trek such an easy and enjoyable one.

From the large display of the trail in the rest area, the path departs into the woods and immediately comes to an interpretive area devoted to multiple-use concept of forests. A sixteen-stop, 30-minute "forest management tour" departs to the right of the display sign, while the trail to Canyon Falls continues on as the left-hand fork, crossing a bridge over Bacco Stream.

Within 0.3 mile you swing by the cola-colored Sturgeon River and arrive at the first falls, a cascade with about a 2-foot drop. Occasionally somebody thinks this is Canyon Falls, but there is no mistaking the real one, which is just another 0.2 mile down the trail. Canyon Falls has an impressive 20-foot drop and marks the beginning of the gorge, which extends west another 0.5 mile along the river. Guard rails have been erected at this point and allow you to lean over the top of the cascade and feel the mist the falling water creates.

At this point there was a "Trail Ends" sign in 1989, but hopefully that is only a temporary solution. The best part of the area is the gorge itself, and the original path can be seen snaking around the huge rock face where the sign is posted. It hugs the gorge and allows you to peer down between the sheer walls of rock to more white water below.

Everybody, especially families with young children, should be extremely careful if they choose to continue to the end of the old trail, a one-way hike of a mile. The original log guard rails are still up, but flimsy and weak in places, and after they end there is nothing between you and the sharp edge of the gorge. But Canyon Gorge is one of the most beautiful gorges in Michigan and a careful walk along the path rewards you with a fascinating view of glacially sculptured rock formations, all set to the turbulent nature of the Sturgeon River.

From the falls, the original path continues another 0.5 mile until it emerges from the gorge and descends to the river's edge just beyond Rapid Falls. To return, look for the path that veers off to the left when you're facing upstream. It swings through the woods, away from the gorge and by-passes Canyon Falls. Along the way, various species of trees have been identified with metal markers about 12 feet up the trunks. This is an excellent opportunity to teach children the differences between yellow and paper birch, and red and white pine. This trail rejoins the main path just west of Bacco Stream.

69. CASCADE FALLS
OTTAWA NATIONAL FOREST

Activity: Day hike
County: Ontonagon
Difficulty: Moderate
Length: 1.8-mile loop
Fee: None
Information: Bergland District office, (906) 575-3441

■ The Cascade Falls hiking trail is a 1.8-mile loop to just one of the Upper Peninsula's many waterfalls. The cascading water is scenic but not as spectacular as Tahquamenon Falls or those seen along Black River Drive (see 73. Black River). What makes this adventure unique and a delight to many children is not the falls but the peaks. Along the Twin Peaks Route of the loop kids climb the side of a rocky ridge to arrive at something of a summit, with a sweeping view of the Trap Hills off in the distance. They do this not once but twice.

The steep climbs are the reason for the moderate rating despite the trail's short length. Children under five or six might have trouble with the Twin Peaks Route, in which case they should stay on the Valley Route, a shorter and considerably easier lowland walk to the falls. Everybody should be wearing boots, especially when hiking over the rocky terrain to the peaks.

From the Forest Service district office in Bergland, head east on M-28 for 1 mile and then north on FR 400 (also labeled FR 222 on some older maps). It's a scenic 7-mile ridge along the dirt road into the heart of the Ottawa National For-

Cascade Falls in Ottawa National Forest

est before you cross a bridge over Cascade Creek and are directed by a sign to turn right for the trailhead.

If planning to hike the entire loop, it's best to start right off with the Twin Peaks Route, while legs are still fresh. The trail is well posted and begins with an immediate ascent toward the top of a rocky bluff. At times it may be difficult to see the path, but in 0.2 mile you should arrive at the first peak, an opening where to the west you see the rugged Trap Hills, while down below is Cascade Creek and the West Branch of the Ontonagon River.

The view is nice but tell the troops it's time to climb the next peak. The trail cuts through a stand of oak, aspen, and hemlock and then resumes climbing. In another quarter mile you reach the second high point, with more good views of the Upper Peninsula's rugged interior. From here it's a rapid descent that levels out somewhat before merging into the Valley Route.

It's only 0.3 mile to the creek. Cascade Falls are small but picturesque and are located on the creek just before it empties into the West Branch. The falls are surrounded by large rocks, where you can sit and listen to the cascading water or watch trout rise in the pool upstream before heading back.

You backtrack to the junction and then head along the Valley Route. This trail is 0.4 mile long and stays entirely in a forest of aspen, balsam, and hemlock. Look for the flattop stumps and other evidence of past timber cutting activities in this area.

70.
LAKE
OF THE CLOUDS
PORCUPINE MOUNTAINS WILDERNESS STATE PARK

Activities: Backpacking, rental cabin
County: Ontonagon
Difficulty: Moderate
Length: 1.5 mile hike round-trip
Fee: Vehicle entry permit, cabin fee
Information: Park headquarters, (906) 885-5275

■ Porcupine Mountains Wilderness State Park is a preserve of 52,000 acres whose secluded lakes, steep ridges, and miles of wild rivers and streams draws a large number of experienced backpackers every summer. The park maintains an 85-mile network of trails that link more than a dozen wilderness cabins and three trailside shelters scattered throughout the heart of the "Porkies," what many consider the only true mountains in Michigan.

As rugged as the Porkies are, the park also offers a number of outdoor adventures for children, and one of the best for young backpackers is an overnight hike to the Lake of the Clouds cabin. The hike to the cabin is short and downhill on the way there and can easily be handled even by children as young as four or five. But the distance between the parking lot above and the lake below is just enough to create an adventurous atmosphere where children feel as though they are spending a night in the "wilderness."

The key to this trip is reserving the cabin. The rustic structures are popular and often reserved a year in advance.

On January 1, park officials begin reserving cabins for the next calender year and often a popular cabin like Lake of the Clouds will be booked solid during a popular month like July within a week or two. Reservations are made either by calling the park headquarters or writing to: Park Manager, Porcupine Mountains Wilderness State Park, 599 M-107, Ontonagon, MI 49953.

The state park, 14 miles west of Ontonagon in the Upper Peninsula, is reached by continuing onto M-107 after M-64 curves to the south at Silver City. The visitor center is reached in 2 miles at the corner of M-107 and South Boundary Road and is open daily from 10:00 A.M. to 6:00 P.M. The center houses an interesting display on the park's wildlife, features slide presentations in its theater, and provides visitors with maps and information on the area.

Continue west another 8 miles along M-107 and the road ends at the parking lot to the Lake of the Clouds overlook, which offers a beautiful panorama of the lake, situated among forested ridges, and the peaks of the Porcupine Mountains. The trailhead is at the east end of the parking lot and is posted "Escarpment Trail." From this trail, you quickly

Lake of the Clouds cabin, Porcupine Mountains Wilderness State Park

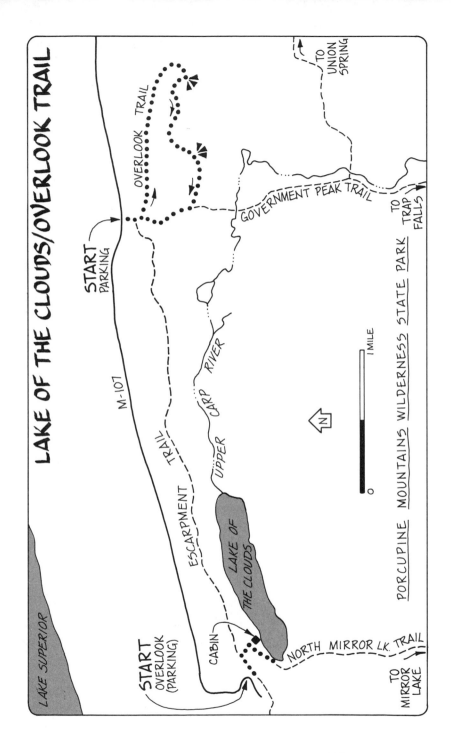

LAKE OF THE CLOUDS/OVERLOOK TRAIL

TO UNION SPRING

OVERLOOK TRAIL

GOVERNMENT PEAK TRAIL

TO TRAP FALLS

START PARKING

M-107

ESCARPMENT TRAIL

UPPER CARP RIVER

LAKE SUPERIOR

LAKE OF THE CLOUDS

CABIN

START OVERLOOK (PARKING)

NORTH MIRROR LK. TRAIL

TO MIRROR LAKE

PORCUPINE MOUNTAINS WILDERNESS STATE PARK

N

0   1 MILE

reach a junction and swing onto North Mirror Lake Trail to begin a rapid descent of switchbacks off the ridge. The 0.5-mile descent ends at a posted junction near the lakeshore, where the water is visible through the trees. To the east the trail leads 0.25 mile to the four-bunk, rustic cabin situated only a few yards from the lakeshore. It comes with a rowboat that can be used during the summer to fish for smallmouth bass and perch.

The western fork of the junction is the North Mirror Lake Trail and the first portion is a scenic and level walk to a long wooden bridge at the west end of Lake of the Clouds. After that the trail becomes much more challenging and often too difficult for young children, as it climbs several ridges on its way to Mirror Lake, a one-way hike of 3.5 miles. The trip back to the car is a hike back up the ridge, an uphill climb to be sure, but a short one that most young kids can endure.

71. OVERLOOK TRAIL
PORCUPINE MOUNTAINS WILDERNESS STATE PARK

Activity: Day hike
County: Ontonagon
Difficulty: Challenging
Length: 3.5-mile loop
Fee: Vehicle entry fee
Information: Park headquarters, (906) 885-5275

■ The Overlook Trail offers one of the few round-trip hikes into the rugged interior of the Porcupine Mountains that is under 10 miles in distance. It begins and ends off of M-107, climbs to the high point of 1,500 feet and passes two viewing points . . . all within a loop of 3.5 miles. This is a challenging hike, however, with long steep climbs and poor footing in many places. It is not for children under seven and everybody should be wearing sturdy hiking boots.

From the visitor's center, the trailhead is 3.5 miles west on M-107 and posted as the "Government Peak Trail." The Peak Trail extends 7.5 miles into the heart of the Porkies, climbs over Government Peak, the second-highest point in the park at 1,850 feet, and ends near Mirror Lake. It also provides access to both ends of the Overlook Trail. Beginning as a wide path, the Peak Trail quickly ascends to a posted junction with the Escarpment Trail, then intersects with the north end of the Overlook Trail, a junction that can be easily missed by those not looking for it.

The Overlook Trail begins by descending to a small stream, climbing out of the gully, and then passing through a wet area for the next 0.3 mile. This ends when the trail enters a stand of stately virgin white pine and hemlock. Impressive trees, especially to children, who have to lean backwards to see the tops of the trunks. They are even more impressed when told that at one time, in the early 1800s, all of Michigan was covered by trees of such size.

At this point the trail may be difficult to follow, as it is not well defined. Keep an eye out for orange diamonds that seem to pop up just when you need them. The trail makes an ascent at 0.6 mile, levels out among the towering pines, and then makes a second ascent at 1.1 miles. This is a steep and steady climb for more than a quarter mile before the trail levels out in a forest of hardwoods and then peaks at 1,500 feet, where it merges with a wide cross-country ski path. The first view is only a short descent away at 1.6 miles and gives way to a glimpse of the park's rugged interior, especially the Escarpment.

From the overlook, you lose much of the height you just worked so hard to gain in a rapid drop with much of it through more virgin pines. At 2.2 miles you come to the second viewing point of the park's interior, though this one is partially obscured by saplings of aspen and oak. The path makes another sharp descent through a stand of pines and at 2.4 miles levels out. Keep an eye out for the orange diamonds, as they will lead you along a level trail the final half mile to the well-marked junction with the Government Peak Trail.

Although the sign says it's 1 mile to M-107 (and your car), tell the tired members of your party it's much closer to a half mile. The trail crosses a wet area that is well planked for a change and then ascends slightly as a wide, unmistakable path. You then descend past the earlier junctions to the trailhead parking area.

72.
UNION
SPRINGS
PORCUPINE MOUNTAINS WILDERNESS STATE PARK

Activity: Backpacking
County: Ontonagon
Difficulty: Easy
Length: 3 miles round-trip
Fee: Vehicle entry fee, camping fee
Information: Park headquarters, (906) 855-5275

■ Michigan's second largest natural spring is the destination for an overnight backpacking trip into Porcupine Mountains that is ideal for children ages five to seven. The trip combines the adventure of spending a night in the park's interior at a trailside campsite, with a view of the bubbling water and swirling sand at the bottom of the spring. Best of all, the walk is surprisingly easy and level considering the rugged reputation of the Porcupine Mountains.

The state park is 14 miles from the city of Ontonagon and is reached by departing M-64 onto M-107. In 2.5 miles, turn left on South Boundary Road and stop at the park visitor center, open 10:00 A.M. to 8:00 P.M. daily during the summer. Here you can view the displays on the wildlife in the area, pick up your backcountry permits, pay the campsite fees, and study a three-dimensional relief map that will quickly dispel any fears the family might have about climbing a "mountain." The hike into Union Springs can be done in tennis shoes, but to go any farther along the trail everybody should be wearing sturdy boots.

The trailhead for Union Springs is another 1.5 miles along South Boundary Road and is posted just past the start of the Union Mine Trail. The walk begins on a forest road that crosses Little Union River and in 0.5 mile comes to a

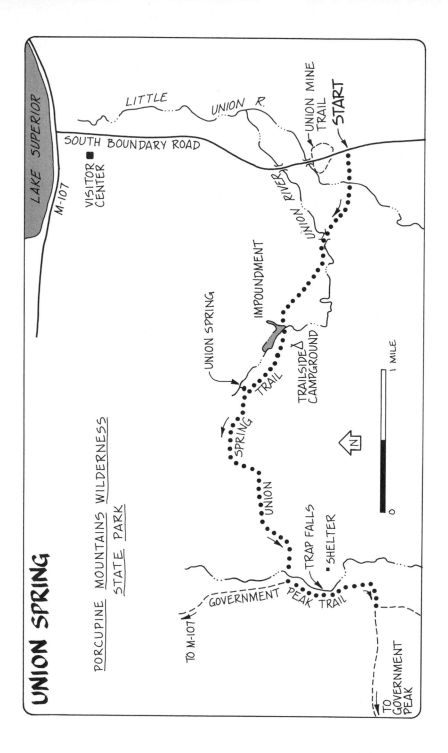

UNION SPRING

PORCUPINE MOUNTAINS WILDERNESS STATE PARK

LAKE SUPERIOR

M-107

LITTLE UNION R.

SOUTH BOUNDARY ROAD

VISITOR CENTER

UNION RIVER

UNION MINE TRAIL

START

IMPOUNDMENT

UNION SPRING

TRAILSIDE CAMPGROUND

SPRING TRAIL

UNION

TRAP FALLS

SHELTER

GOVERNMENT PEAK TRAIL

TO M-107

TO GOVERNMENT PEAK

N

1 MILE

0

locked gate. Beyond the gate the forest closes in as the trail crosses a bridge over Union River and then begins a short ascent, the only climb of the day.

Within a mile you come to a sign directing you to make a sharp swing west, after which the trail arrives at the impoundment, a large pond making for a scenic setting. The trailside campground, on the other side of the trail, consists of two tent pads and fire rings.

The impoundment is stocked with brook trout each spring and it's obvious from the beaten path along the shoreline that most people fish for brook trout just off the trail along the south end. Fishing is good in May and early June but sporadic after that. Most anglers use small spinners—Mepps No. 0 through No. 2 are popular choices—and tip them with a leaf worm or a piece of a nightcrawler.

Union Spring is another 0.5 mile farther west. The trail remains a level forest walk but can be wet at times. It's well marked by orange and yellow diamonds and it doesn't take long to reach the spring and the viewing platform at one end of the pool. The end of the platform, usually under water, puts you right over the place where 700 gallons of water bubble out of the ground each minute.

For those looking for a longer overnight trip, continue west on the trail and in 2 miles you come to the junction with Government Peak Trail. Head south (left) to arrive at a trailside shelter with bunks, where backpackers can stay on a first-come-first-serve basis. The shelter is located near Trap Falls.

73. BLACK RIVER
OTTAWA NATIONAL FOREST

Activities: Scenic drive, day hike
County: Gogebic
Difficulty: Easy to moderate
Length: One-way trails vary from 0.2 to 0.8 miles
Fee: None
Information: Bessemer District Office, (906) 667-0261

■ Perhaps more than mountains, large tracts of wilderness, or the icy waters of Lake Superior, the trademark of the Upper Peninsula is waterfalls. There are hundreds of cascades in the Upper Peninsula, as opposed to a pair in the Lower Peninsula, and they include such well-known leaps as Tahquamenon Falls, the third largest east of the Mississippi, or Munising Falls, set in a rock amphitheater where visitors can walk behind the cascade. But the best collection of falling white water is found along Black River Drive (also labeled CR 513) in the western end of the Upper Peninsula.

Departing from Bessemer, the paved road heads north for 15 miles to end at Black River Harbor, one of the few access points to Lake Superior and the site of a National Forest campground. It's a scenic drive past high rocky bluffs and the rugged hills that have made Bessemer a haven for skiers during the winter. But the high point of the trip are five waterfalls all located a short walk from the road.

The cascades are linked together by a portion of the North Country Trail, which hikers can walk from Cooper Peak Ski Flying Hill to the campground, a 5.5-mile trip. But it's more convenient for traveling families and enjoyable for young children if you drive the road, stopping at the trailhead of each individual falls. The hikes are short, the longest being a 1.5-mile round-trip, and the trails well marked and maintained. While they can be walked in tennis shoes, they do include a number of long staircases and for that reason visiting all five falls makes for an adventure of moderate difficulty.

GREAT CONGLOMERATE FALLS

This is the first falls, located 12 miles north of US-2 in Bessemer. The trail is a one-way walk of 0.8 miles and begins as a level forest walk for 0.5 mile, then drops steadily to the posted junction with the North Country Recreation Trail. Near the junction is an overview of the falls, really two falls with a 40-foot drop and split in half by a huge rock face. For a little added adventure, you send half your party north along the North Country Trail to reach the next set of cascades, the Potawatomi and Gorge Falls, in 0.5 mile. The others return to the car and drive to the next trailhead.

POTAWATOMI AND GORGE FALLS

The posted trailhead is another mile along Black River Road and marks the entrance to both falls. The best way to view them is to begin with the trail to Potawatomi Falls and then hike along the river a short way to Gorge Falls before returning to the parking area. The loop is a 0.8-mile walk. The trail quickly passes a junction to the North Country Trail and then emerges at a view of the Potawatomi Falls, a cascade 130 feet wide with a 30-foot drop.

Gorge Falls is only 800 feet downriver, but the trail passes five observation platforms with the first providing the best view of Potawatomi Falls. The fourth one is the most spectacular, however, putting you right over the 24-foot drop of Gorge Falls and providing an excellent view of the rock canyon the Black River has carved over time. No two waterfalls are alike and nowhere is that better seen than here. The Gorge is a narrow drop of thundering water while the Potawatomi is a spread-out veil flowing over a rock embankment.

SANDSTONE FALLS

It's another mile north along Black River Road to reach the posted trailhead of this small falls. The 0.2-mile trail is basically a long staircase descent to the river, where you can scramble over large red rocks to stand almost directly over the falls and feel the rise of cool mist on your face. Although Sandstone Falls is not a large cascade, the area is intriguing to children when they are shown the various rock formations and hollows carved out of the sandstone and conglomerate rock by centuries of rushing water.

RAINBOW FALLS

A half mile from the campground or 14.5 miles from US-2, you reach the posted trailhead of Rainbow Falls. The 0.5-mile trail extends from the parking area to a long and somewhat steep stairway that ends at an observation platform above the cascade with a 40-foot drop. The falls pick up their name from the mist that often reflects rainbows with the right angle of sunlight. The platform also provides an excellent view of the final leg of the Black River before it empties into Lake Superior.

74.
CLARK
LAKE

SYLVANIA WILDERNESS AND RECREATION AREA

Activities: Canoeing, fishing
County: Gogebic
Difficulty: Moderate
Length: 2- to 3-day trip
Fee: None
Information: Watersmeet Ranger District, (906) 358-4551

■ Sylvania Recreation Area is a federally designated wilderness located in the remote western corner of the Upper Peninsula on the Michigan-Wisconsin border. The 21,000-acre preserve is a beautiful combination of maple, birch, hemlock, and scattered pine forest, much of it stands of virgin timber broken up only by the crystal clear water of more than thirty lakes. Many claim the water quality of the lakes is better than in almost any other region of the country and often it's possible to lean over the side of a canoe and see the bottom more than 30 feet below.

Clark Lake is the largest and deepest one in Sylvania and makes for an ideal overnight canoeing trip. Families who do not want to deal with portaging a boat can paddle the lake to one of its six wilderness-type campsites for an enjoyable adventure that still allows you to escape the sights and sounds of modern society. Most campsites have tables, tent pads, fire grills, and vault toilets. In all there are eighty-four such campsites scattered throughout Sylvania and those looking for a more challenging trip can portage in one of three directions from Clark Lake's south end.

Access to the area is by US-2. At the corner of US-2 and US-45, just south of Watersmeet, is the Sylvania Visitor Center (906-358-4724) that has maps, information, and an interpretive display area devoted to the wilderness. From the visitor center head west on US-2 for 4 miles and then south on Country Road 535. The entrance off Country Road 535 is

Clark Lake, Sylvania Wilderness and Recreation Area

marked and near it is an information station where visitors fill out backcountry permits and sign up for a campsite.

Use of the campsites is by permit only and handed out on a first-come, first-serve basis. Families entering the area should be prepared to carry in all their drinking water or be able to treat lake water for *Giardia lamblia*. Also remember this is bear country and that food should never be kept in tents. Store extra food in a cache suspended by rope between two trees.

Parking and a boat launch are located at the north end of Clark Lake and from there it's a 2.5-mile paddle to its south end. There's no white water to worry about—that's what makes wilderness lakes the ideal first canoe adventure for children—but occasionally the wind will whip up the surface and create choppy conditions. If that's the case, just wait until late afternoon when an evening calm generally settles in.

The first spot to pitch a tent, Ash campsite, is less than a half-mile paddle away on the east shore. But the best destination for a sense of isolation in the woods is Birch campsite. This site is situated on its own bay formed by a long, bent peninsula extending into the middle of the lake. The 2.5-mile paddle to the campsite can be cut down considerably by por-

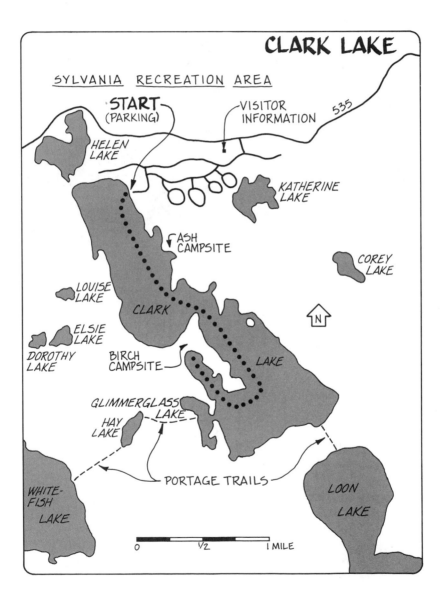

taging from the sandy beach on the north side of the arm to the bay on the south side.

Nearby is the narrow gap into Glimmerglass Lake and the entire southwest corner of the lake is an excellent area to fish for bass. Sylvania has special fishing regulations (consult a Michigan Fishing Guide for all rules), which include not keeping any bass, regardless of the size, and not using live bait. Young anglers might find the change from a bobber and worm frustrating at first, but a trip into Clark Lake is an excellent opportunity to show them that, yes, bright metal spinners and beads do catch fish. With a child in the front of the canoe casting, maneuver the boat along the shore and have him or her cast among the many fallen trees and deadheads along shore. Do this on a still evening near dusk and it won't take long for smallmouth bass to hit the lure and put on an impressive acrobatic show with several leaps out of the water.

Man, oh man, no bluegill ever fought like that. Sacrifice one evening of fishing to paddle the canoe for your son or daughter, and you'll have a fishing partner for life.

75. LAKE WHITTLESEY
ISLE ROYALE NATIONAL PARK

Activity: Canoeing
County: Keweenaw
Difficulty: Moderate
Length: 6- to 8-day trip
Fee: Ferry transport fees
Information: Park headquarters in Houghton, (906) 482-0984

■ Isle Royale National Park has the most adventurous beginning of any wilderness trip in Michigan. Departing from Houghton on the Keweenaw Peninsula, campers, backpackers, and canoeists scramble aboard the large, and very blue,

Ranger III. Slowly the boat pulls away from the dock with most children hanging onto the rails to watch the town, drawbridge, and finally the land slip away. For the next 5 hours there is nothing but water to look at and then suddenly a line of dark green appears on the horizon and Isle Royale emerges from the world of blue.

By the time children arrive at Isle Royale they feel as though they were deep in the heart of wilderness. And they are. Isle Royale, Michigan's only national park, is also the state's most pristine wilderness, supporting such wildlife as loons, moose, and wolves. Most people regard the island and its 170-mile network of trails as a rugged backpacking trip. But the ferry transport around the park can be utilized for a week-long canoeing adventure of only moderate difficulty. This trip involves a pair of half-mile portages, but the paddles between campsites are short and the water well protected.

The key is arranging the transport on ferries. From Michigan, you can reach the island park with a canoe from Houghton on board the *Ranger III* (906-482-0984) or from Copper Harbor on the *Isle Royale Queen* (906-482-4950 winter, 906-289-4437 summer). Ferry reservations to the island should be in advance, as the boats often fill up. The *Ranger III* begins accepting dates by mail the first of March and over the phone in April.

Bring not only a canoe, paddles, and lifejackets, but pack in watertight bags (garbage bags if nothing else), tent, sleeping bags, all the food you will need, a water filter, and a small campstove, as fires are not allowed at most backcountry campsites. Plan the first night at Rock Harbor, the bustling park headquarters at the east end of the island, where you can attend a backcountry orientation and pick up the necessary permit. You will also be able to make arrangements that night with the captain of the ferry, *Voyageur,* which will arrive at the harbor after 5:00 P.M. Monday, Wednesday, and Saturday from late May through early September.

By purchasing a Rock-Harbor-to-Windigo ticket and putting your canoe on the boat, you can use the ferry to bypass the long 9.5-mile paddle down Rock Harbor as well as the 2-mile portage into Lake Richie, the longest in the park. The ticket will allow you to be dropped off at Chippewa Har-

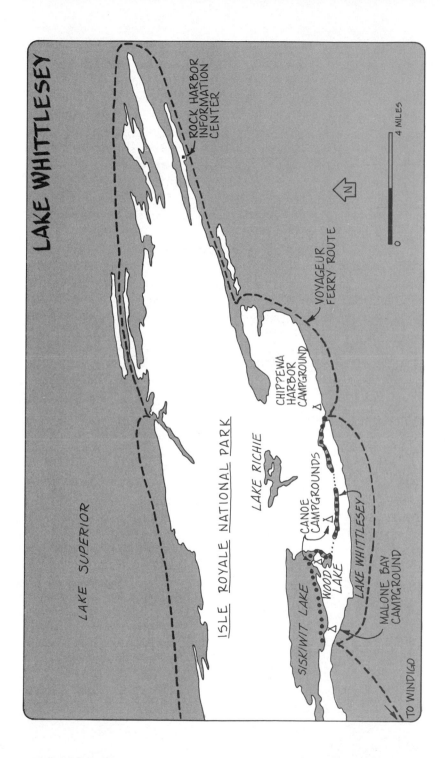

LAKE WHITTLESEY

LAKE SUPERIOR

ROCK HARBOR INFORMATION CENTER

ISLE ROYALE NATIONAL PARK

LAKE RICHIE

CHIPPEWA HARBOR CAMPGROUND

VOYAGEUR FERRY ROUTE

N

0   4 MILES

SISKIWIT LAKE

CANOE CAMPGROUNDS

WOOD LAKE

LAKE WHITTLESEY

MALONE BAY CAMPGROUND

TO WINDIGO

bor on Tuesday, Thursday, or Sunday and spend a night at the scenic campground situated high above the water. The first paddle would be the length of Chippewa Harbor and then the 0.6-mile portage into Lake Whittlesey.

Whittlesey is a narrow body of water that stretches almost 2 miles and is broken up at the east end by a pencil-thin island. The canoe campground is located on the north shore, well past the island, and is a visible clearing from the water. You'll find tent pads, vault toilets, but most of all, seclusion, a true wilderness setting. The lake can be fished for walleye and northern pike or just be a place to sit in the canoe at dusk to watch for moose.

The following day would be a short paddle to the portage to Wood Lake, a hike of 0.6 mile. The trail emerges at the southeast corner of the lake and from there it's a 0.5-mile paddle straight across to the large cove on the west side, site of the next canoe campground. The third and final day in the canoe would be a 3.5-mile paddle from Wood Lake to the portage to Malone Bay campground. If the weather is good, plan on 2 to 3 hours to make the trip, longer if the wind is against you.

Make arrangements ahead of time to complete your adventure to Isle Royale by picking up the *Voyageur* when it passes through on Tuesday, Thursday, or Sunday. You'll spend at least one night at Windigo, two if you arrive on Thursday, before the *Voyageur* returns from Grand Portage, Minnesota, and takes you around the other side of the island to Rock Harbor, where ferries will return you to Michigan. Although the cost of ferry tickets can add up quickly for a family, this trip provides a good view of the island from each shoreline, plus a 3 day-4 night canoe trip of easy paddling in one of the most isolated sections of the park.

QUICK REFERENCE TO THE ADVENTURES

SPECIAL ACTIVITIES:

1 Shipwreck
2 Lighthouse
3 Ghost towns
4 Beachcombing
5 Rafting
6 Rock climbing
7 Snowshoeing
8 Luge run

	Recommended age (−3, +3, +6, +9)	Camping	Day hikes/backpacking (D/B)	Climbing "mountains"	Bicycling	Canoeing	Skiing	Scenic drive/cruise (D/C)	Birding	Interpretive centers	Frontier cabins	Fishing	Special activities
SOUTHEAST MICHIGAN													
1. Walk-in-the-Water Canoe Trail	+3	9				•		C		•			
2. Maybury Living Farm	+6				•			•		•			
3. Wildwing Lake	+3		D							•			
4. Huron Swamp	+6		D		•			•		•			
5. Paint Creek	+6		D							•			
6. Graham Lakes	+6												
7. Crooked Lake	+3		D					•		•		•	
8. Roston Cabin	−3							•			•		
HEARTLAND													
9. Huron River	+3	•				•							
10. Potawatomi Trail	+9		B										
11. Bog Trail	+3		D							•			
12. Graves Hill	+3		D	•									
13. Hudson Mills	+6				•								
14. The Ledges	+3		D							•			6
15. Hoister Lake	+6	•	D										
16. Rent-A-Tipi	−3	•											
17. Silver Creek Pathway	+3	•	D										
18. Marl Lake	+6		D						•				
LAKE HURON													
19. Sanilac Petroglyphs	+3		D										
20. Huron Sand Dunes	+6	•	D										
21. Perch Charters	+6											•	
22. Shiawassee Waterfowl Trail	+6		D						•				

	Recommended age (−3, +3, +6, +9)	Camping	Day hikes/backpacking (D/B)	Climbing "mountains"	Bicycling	Canoeing	Skiing	Scenic drive/cruise (D/C)	Birding	Interpretive centers	Frontier cabins	Fishing	Special activities
23. Highbanks Trail	+6		D				•			•			
24. Reid Lake	+6		B									•	
25. Jewell Lake	+3	•	D										
26. Kirtland's Warbler Tour	+6								•	•			
27. Negwegon Beach Trail	+6		D										
28. Bell Townsite	+3		D										1,3
29. Sinkholes	+6		D										
30. New Presque Isle Lighthouse	+3		D										2
31. Ocqueoc Falls	+6		D										
LAKE MICHIGAN													
32. Backroads Bikeways	+9				•					•			•
33. Warren Woods	+6		D										
34. Love Creek	+6		D				•			•			7
35. Michigan Fisheries Interpretive Center	+3									•			
36. Mount Baldhead	+3		D	•									
37. Dune Overlook	+3		D							•			
38. Luge Run	+6						•						8
39. Silver Lake Sand Dunes	+6		D										
40. Bowman Lake	+3		B,D										
41. Nordhouse Dunes	+6		B										
42. Michigan Trail	+6	•	D										
NORTHWEST MICHIGAN													
43. Platte Plains Trail	+3		B										
44. Pierce Stocking Drive	−3							D					
45. Dune Climb	+3		D										
46. Good Harbor Bay Ski Trail	+6						•						
47. South Mantiou Island	+6		B										1,2
48. Chain O'Lakes	+6	•	D				•						
49. Sand Lakes	+6		B										
50. Skegemog Swamp	+3		D							•			

	Recommended age (−3, +3, +6, +9)	Camping	Day hikes/backpacking (D/B)	Climbing "mountains"	Bicycling	Canoeing	Skiing	Scenic drive/cruise (D/C)	Birding	Interpretive centers	Frontier cabins	Fishing	Special activities
51. Au Sable River Foot Trail	+3		D										
52. Forbush Corners, Green Trail	+6		B,D				•						
52. Forbush Corners, Pines Trail	+9		B,D										
53. Deadmans Hill	+3		B,D										
54. Petoskey Stones	−3	•											4
55. Nebo Trail	+6		B				•			•			
56. Mount Nebo and Big Stone Creek	+3		D	•									

EASTERN UPPER PENINSULA

	Recommended age (−3, +3, +6, +9)	Camping	Day hikes/backpacking (D/B)	Climbing "mountains"	Bicycling	Canoeing	Skiing	Scenic drive/cruise (D/C)	Birding	Interpretive centers	Frontier cabins	Fishing	Special activities
57. Big Knob and Crow Lake	+3	•	D	•									
58. Marshland Wildlife Drive	−3							D					
59. Au Sable Light Station	+3	•	D										1,2
60. Pictured Rocks	−3							C					
61. Kitchi-Iti-Kipi Spring	−3							C					
62. Ninga Aki Pathway	+3	•	D										
63. Klondike Lake	+6					•						•	
64. Tyoga Townsite	+3	•	D										3

WESTERN UPPER PENINSULA

	Recommended age (−3, +3, +6, +9)	Camping	Day hikes/backpacking (D/B)	Climbing "mountains"	Bicycling	Canoeing	Skiing	Scenic drive/cruise (D/C)	Birding	Interpretive centers	Frontier cabins	Fishing	Special activities
65. Piers Gorge	+6		D										5
66. Sugarloaf Mountain	+3		D	•									
67. Craig Lake	+6		B			•					•		
68. Canyon Falls and Gorge	+3		D										
69. Cascade Falls	+3		D	•									
70. Lake of the Clouds	+3		B								•		
71. Overlook Trail	+9		D										
72. Union Springs	+3		B										
73. Black River	+3		D					D					
74. Clark Lake	+3				•							•	
75. Lake Whittlesey	+6				•								

INDEX

Jim DuFresne, a resident of Clarkston, Michigan, is the author of *Kidventures*, a popular column on outdoor activities for families. He has hiked extensively around the world and has shared many of his outdoor adventures with his two children, ages 4 and 7. He is the author of many books on the outdoors, including *Michigan State Parks* (The Mountaineers) and *Michigan: Off the Beaten Path* (Globe Pequot).